Luck Is No Accident

LUCK Is No ACCIDENT

Second Edition

*Making the Most of Happenstance
in Your Life and Career*

John D. Krumboltz, Ph.D.
Al S. Levin, Ed.D.

Impact Publishers®
ATASCADERO, CALIFORNIA

ATTENTION ORGANIZATIONS AND CORPORATIONS:
This book is available at quantity discounts on bulk purchases for educational, business, or sales promotional use. For further information, please contact Impact Publishers, P.O. Box 6016, Atascadero, California 93423-6016. Phone 805-466-5917, e-mail: info@impactpublishers.com

Library of Congress Cataloging-in-Publication Data

Krumboltz, John D.
  Luck is no accident : making the most of happenstance in your life and career / John D. Krumboltz, Al S. Levin. — 2nd ed.
    p. cm.
  Includes bibliographical references and index.
  ISBN 978-1-886230-03-3 (alk. paper)
  1. Vocational guidance. 2. Chance. 3. Fortune. 4. Career development. 5. Success in business. I. Levin, Al S. II. Title.
  HF5381.K739 2010
    650.1—dc22   2010017833

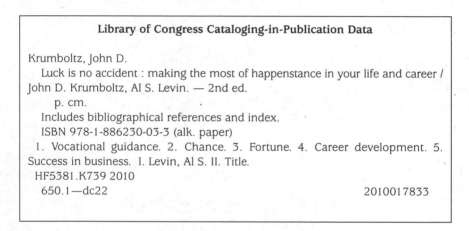

Impact Publishers and colophon are registered trademarks of Impact Publishers, Inc.

Cover design by
K.A. White Design, San Luis Obispo, California
Adapted by Gayle Downs, Gayle Force Design, Atascadero, California
Printed in the United States of America on acid-free, recycled paper.
Published by
Impact  Publishers®
POST OFFICE BOX 6016
ATASCADERO, CALIFORNIA 93423-6016
www.impactpublishers.com

Contents

Acknowledgements

We wish to gratefully acknowledge the work of Dr. Kathleen Mitchell of City College of San Francisco who initially brought the three of us together to discuss how unplanned events are influential in everyone's career. Dr. Mitchell is to be credited for the term and the career counseling theory, Planned Happenstance. The three of us shared ideas and opinions in frequent meetings over three years. Kathleen convinced us of the necessity to change the current paradigm of career counseling to better meet the needs of today's workplace. The three of us collaborated in presenting symposia and workshops at career development conferences. Dr. Mitchell is the first author of an article in which we spelled out the details from our deliberations and their implications for counselors.

We are also indebted to Diane Byster and Anne Chan for their detailed feedback on preliminary drafts of the manuscript and for contributing stories of how their careers were also influenced by unplanned events.

Hundreds of people have contributed their own personal stories which have helped us to crystallize our ideas of how creating luck actually works in practice. While we were not able to include all these stories in the book, we have benefited from the wisdom in all the stories. We have promised anonymity to many who were willing to have their stories published, and we have occasionally taken literary license to modify names and places to disguise the identity of contributors.

Al would like to thank his wife and daughter, Eileen and Rachel, for always keeping an eye out for good happenstance illustrations. John is grateful to his wife, Betty, and to his children, Ann, Jenny, Shauna and Scott for living lives filled with multiple stories which helped to inspire this book.

Introduction

This book can help you create a more satisfying life for yourself. What makes one's life satisfying? Philosophers have debated the "meaning of life" question for centuries. Our answer is that there is no *one* way in which life is made more meaningful...there are *multiple* ways. And what seems satisfying at age twelve is different at age thirty, and fifty, and ninety-nine, and perhaps on every day in between. Some of the most important components of a meaningful and satisfying life would include the following:

- Contributing to others' health or welfare
- Creating useful products and services
- Solving challenging problems
- Earning income sufficient for your needs
- Meeting personal needs
- Protecting the natural environment
- Sharing camaraderie with other workers
- Behaving ethically and respectfully
- Having exciting experiences
- Appreciating the miracle of life
- Sharing relationships of love and respect
- Maintaining health and fitness
- Marveling at the beauty of the environment that surrounds us

Many of the events in our lives are influenced by unplanned and unexpected events. We can call it "good luck" or "bad luck," however, we are convinced that "Luck Is No Accident."

Each of us plays a key role in creating unexpected career- and life-enhancing events and transforming them into real opportunities. Although this book concentrates on career-related activities, we see that creating opportunities from unexpected events is a crucial part of creating every component of a meaningful and satisfying life.

The first edition of this book struck a chord with a number of our readers; producing a second edition created the opportunity for us to address the many questions that they raised.

Creating benefits from unexpected events can be accomplished by the poverty-stricken unemployed as well as by billionaires. We have added stories from those who grew up in poverty under harsh conditions.

Economic recessions, wars, hurricanes, and forest fires are examples of major negative events to which individuals must adapt as positively as they can. We acknowledge that unexpected events happen not only to individuals but also to industries, cities, nations, and the world.

Recognition that climate change can be affected by human actions has influenced us to add a section and references on green careers.

The widespread use of the Internet has inspired us to add a sampling of websites helpful for beginning to explore much useful information.

You will find here:
- Real-life stories that illustrate that *luck is no accident*;
- Specific advice based on these stories that you will be able to apply to your own life; and
- Thought-provoking and action-oriented exercises that you can use right now.

The story behind the title of this book is an illustration of the fact that "luck is no accident." Surprisingly, one of the most difficult tasks in writing a book is coming up with a good title. The title needs to capture the main theme of the book in just a few words, and it must be understandable and, preferably, catchy as well. We struggled for many months with different possibilities. As we were about to tell our editor, Dr. Bob Alberti, about our final title idea, he said to us with a hint of desperation: "I think this might be number sixty-three!"

Al Levin's true story about how the title of this book came to be provides a good example of why "Luck is No Accident."

My wife Eileen, our daughter Rachel, and I decided to go to dinner at a local restaurant that we frequent. When we arrived we were greeted by the hostess, who told us it would be five minutes or so before we could be seated. As we waited, Eileen glanced up on the wall and noticed a plaque with the inscription "Success is No Accident: Safety First Award — 2001." She immediately turned to me and said "How about something like that as a title for your book? You know, 'Luck is No Accident.'" I loved it immediately.

Some people would simply call this incident "pure luck." We look at it quite differently. There were actions that were taken that led to a new title that everyone liked. What wisdom can we glean from this example of "luck?"

Be aware of your surroundings.
- Eileen had her eyes open to the environment around her, even in a place as mundane as a frequently visited restaurant.

Take a risk, even with rejection as a possible outcome.
- Despite the fact that he had rejected other title ideas she had proposed, Eileen told Al about her discovery.

Be adaptable and open-minded.
- Eileen adapted the inscription to better match the concept of the book.
- The co-authors and publisher were open-minded about the new title idea, although it was getting late in the game.

You're probably reading this book now because you have a problem you wish to solve. Unhappy with your job? Don't have a job? Facing a difficult career or life decision? Wishing for that "lucky break"? This book will teach you how you can create your own luck and benefit from it.

You will read stories about well-known people as well as average everyday people who provide proof that luck is no accident. We believe everyone has a similar story to tell. Our wish for you is to be able to write your own good-luck story after you finish this book.

Chapter 1

Make the Most of Unplanned Events

*Things turn out best for people who make the best of the way
things turn out.*
> — Art Linkletter

*None of us knows what the next change is going to be,
what unexpected opportunity is just around the corner.*
> — Kathleen Norris

*Success is getting what you want; happiness is wanting what
you get.*
> — Ingrid Bergman

Have you ever noticed that unplanned events — chance occurrences — more often determine your life and career choices than all the careful planning you do? A chance meeting, a broken appointment, a spontaneous vacation trip, a "fill-in" job, a newly discovered hobby — these are the kinds of experiences — *happenstances* — that lead to unexpected life directions and career choices.

In this book we're encouraging you to take actions to open up opportunities even when you don't know the outcomes, to take advantage of chance events, to keep your options open, and to make the most of what life offers. We are not opposed to planning, but we don't think you should stick with a plan that is not working for you anymore.

Adapting to Changes in the Economy, Technology, and Government

Unexpected events happen not only to individuals, they also happen to communities, nations, and the world. Hurricanes strike, wars break out, financial institutions go bankrupt, the world's economy shrinks. What can you do when forces beyond your control affect your life?

There are no easy answers, but if the world around you is changing, you must be ready to change too. Here are ten simple ideas (in no particular order) to get you started.

1. Be open to considering a completely different kind of work that may well require you to learn a whole new set of skills. Don't think that you must continue the same kind of work you had before you were laid off.

2. Be willing to accept a job that pays less than your previous job. It is better to have a job than no job.

3. When you apply for a job, you will be asked, "What kind of work do you want to do?" Don't answer that question. Say instead, "I want to help make your company become more successful. What problems are you having? Let's see how I can help solve them."

4. Sell items that you no longer need. eBay Inc. is one company that provides an easy method for disposing of unwanted items at fair prices. It does take effort to learn the skills, but many people have learned how to buy and sell profitably.

5. Keep learning wherever you go. If you accept a low-paying job, learn from your supervisor. Find out what the supervisor needs to succeed. Help your supervisor become successful. You will become a more valuable employee in the process and may someday become the supervisor yourself.

6. Keep tuned in to changes that may provide opportunities. For example, the threat of climate change has spurred

many companies to expand into "green" mode. The internet is filled with green job listings. An emerging field like this can provide intriguing opportunities for learning and advancement. See the list of websites in the bibliography.

7. Simplify your diet. You may like a steak dinner at a fancy restaurant better than eating a simple meal at home, but preparing your own nutritious dinner at home is a lot cheaper and often healthier, too.

8. Be willing to move to a new location. If your community has few if any job opportunities, consider moving somewhere else. Don't get stuck in the mud. Explore possibilities carefully before you move. Maybe just one family member at a time needs to explore an alternative location.

9. Explore practical learning experiences. Community colleges offer a variety of career-related training programs. But remember when you graduate, all you receive is a piece of paper called a diploma. You don't get a job offer. It's smart to find out the job-finding experiences of previous graduates before committing yourself to an expensive training program.

10. Avoid internet scams. Scam artists have developed intriguing ways of enticing unwary internet users into parting with their money. Be skeptical of anything that seems too good to be true.

Unexpected events take place throughout our lives. Many events that affect your life actually took place long before you were born. For example, you had no role in choosing your parents, native language, ethnicity, or birthplace. How much control did you have in choosing your first school, your classmates, your teachers? You might think that you had the opportunity to choose your friends, when in actuality most people become friends when they happen to be in close proximity of one another through a neighborhood, school, work, or family connections.

Blondie By Young & Drake

Make the most of your present situation.

How about your career? Have unexpected events affected your major field in school, your occupation, your employers, your co-workers, your supervisors? We all like to believe that we freely chose our occupations, but think about all the events and circumstances that exposed us to a limited set of alternatives. Did you choose your employer, or did your employer choose you? Few people have the opportunity to choose their own co-workers or supervisors.

You may be wondering if there really is anything you can control. The good news is that you can control *the actions that you take and how you react to positive and negative experiences*. And those are powerful factors in determining the directions your life takes.

Some books promise that if you can just identify your life's passion, state a career goal, determine your personality type, or even consider your astrological sign, you will find the key to the perfect job, career, lifestyle, or mate. Those books don't account for the unpredictability of life. You will continue to be influenced by the people and events that you encounter, often by chance, including your family, friends, the economy, and changes in technology. No one can predict the future. Unexpected events are inevitable. But if you are alert, you can make the most of them when they happen.

You have control over your own actions and how you think about the events that impact your life. None of us can control the outcomes, but your actions can increase the probability that desired outcomes will occur. There are no guarantees in life. The only guarantee is that doing nothing will get you nowhere.

Take Advantage of Unexpected Disappointments

Unplanned events are sometimes positive, sometimes negative. Both positive and negative events offer opportunities. Here we see how Claire capitalized on a disappointment.

Bumped Off a Flight — and Into a Career

I was working at a job in San Francisco that didn't interest me anymore. I was bored, tired, and needed a change. It was time to take my annual vacation. I bought a plane ticket and was all set to go. While at the airport, waiting for my plane, I was bumped off of my flight. I was disappointed that my vacation plans had been disrupted, but the airline gave me credit for another ticket that was good anywhere for one year. Instead of going anywhere, I stayed home.

About a year later, I remembered that my airplane ticket credit was about to expire. Aha, this would be a good time to quit my job and take some time off. I had always wanted to visit the Boston area, especially Harvard. During my trip I was walking around the Harvard campus when I decided to visit a few academic departments to learn about research opportunities. I was even able to drop in on the department chair of one of these departments. I learned that he needed a research assistant who was fluent in Spanish. He also was looking for someone who lived in Northern California near UC Berkeley, had a car, was available in the mornings, and was interested in immigration policy. I had all of those requirements. I was able to explain all this to the professor and my brief drop-in visit turned into two hours. I was offered and accepted the position that day. Was this a coincidence? Divine intervention? Who knows? It has been a perfect match and I couldn't be happier. Had I come one week earlier or one week later, the opportunity wouldn't have been available.

The fact that Claire was bumped from her flight was a chance event that interrupted her plans. There was no way she could have predicted the consequences a year later. Note, however, that she played a major role in making the desirable consequences happen:

- She used the compensatory airline ticket to visit the Harvard campus.
- She used her time there contacting professors in her field of interest.
- When she found an opportunity, she sold the professor on her qualifications and interest.

Claire could have spent the time shopping, visiting museums or sleeping in her hotel room. Instead, she took constructive steps to convert an aborted airline flight into a fascinating job opportunity.

Terrible catastrophes affect many lives — often in unexpected ways. Even in the worst of conditions there are ways to become engaged in constructive activities. Let's see how Elena created her own opportunities.

At the Worst Moment of My Life...

I had gone to graduate school in Italy to improve my knowledge of international issues so I could further my career in television news. I wanted to be a foreign affairs producer and had been completely focused on my career up to that time. In Italy, I was in a very bad accident and nearly died. I ended up in the hospital for surgery. On my first day in the hospital the first English-speaking person I met was a Bosnian soldier who had been injured in the war in Bosnia. We were the same age, and there, at the worst moment of my life, I met someone who was so much worse off that there was no way for me not to survive my ordeal with courage. I stayed in Italy and finished school.

I lost track of him in the hospital, but three years later I traced him through the American Red Cross (where I had volunteered after graduate school) and I realized my true desire was to help refugees. I started a fund-raiser for him and his family and raised a few thousand dollars that I sent directly to him.

Gradually since then, I have evolved into thinking that the best way to do something I love (producing film/video) for a cause that I love (helping refugees) is to volunteer my time for non-profit groups and make promotional films to further their cause. I have since become involved with a relief group that does work in an area I really believe in, and I have been organizing a fund-raiser for them to go to refugees in Kosovo. I have also been taking film classes and meeting independent filmmakers.

When Elena thought about her life in comparison to that of a seriously injured Bosnian soldier, she realized that she had a great deal to be thankful for and could use the experience to inspire her own actions:

- She finished school.
- She traced the soldier through the Red Cross.
- She started a fundraiser for him.
- She volunteered to work for non-profit refugee organizations.
- She made promotional films.
- She took additional film classes.
- She continued networking with other independent filmmakers.

Be Open to Changing Locations and Occupations

Some people feel that they are stuck in an unsatisfactory job because they have to remain in the same location and in the same type of industry. Good interpersonal and communication skills are needed in almost every type of work. Other technical skills can be learned on the job. You don't need to restrict yourself to one location or occupation just because that is your experience so far. Consider Dianna's case.

"I Can Do That!" — Old Skills Fit a New Industry

I worked in the entertainment industry and had what most people considered a very good job. I was going places at a young age. However, I was extremely stressed out and overworked by the age of twenty-five.

Then my husband had an opportunity to move to another city with his job. We discussed it and decided to go. I left an upwardly mobile job for no job. After moving across the country I looked for another job in the entertainment industry for several months without any success.

Then one day my husband brought home a job description of a position in the training department of his information technology company. The job required many of the same skills that I had been using. I didn't know much about information technology, but the job required me to prepare curriculum materials (it was like writing a script) and teach new workers (it was like acting a role). It was a completely different job, but I persuaded them that I could learn whatever else I needed to know.

I applied and was hired. It has turned out to be very rewarding. I am much happier and much less stressed out. I like what I do very much.

Dianna gave up her job to accompany her husband across the country. She tried to find another job in the same industry she had left without success. Then she took some major actions:

- She responded to a job announcement in an unrelated industry.
- She saw how the skills she had developed previously could apply to the new job.
- She convinced the employer that she could learn whatever else she needed to learn.

Share Your Interests and Experiences with People You Meet

It is amazing to discover how many people actually want to help you if they know something about you. Don't be bashful about sharing your desires, concerns and experiences with others. You may find valuable contacts in the least expected spots as Alysha discovered.

Roommate Wanted — Job Found

Soon after arriving in Chicago, I was looking for a place to live by answering "roommate wanted" ads. I responded to one of the ads which was placed by a French teacher. Upon learning that I had majored in French, she told me that she was vacating a position as a summer school teacher of French and that the position was still open. I contacted the school, interviewed, and got the job.

When the regular teacher returned at the end of the summer, she told me that the school where she had taught previously needed substitutes. I applied and was called on a frequent basis. While there, I learned of another school that had a vacancy in the French Department. I applied and although I didn't have a credential, I got the job on the condition that I get one, which I did.

Alysha was not bashful about sharing her experiences and desires with others. She took concrete actions to uncover opportunities:

- She responded to a roommate ad.
- She conducted an informal information interview with the roommate.
- She learned about a job opening, applied, interviewed and got the job.
- When that job ended, she did substitute teaching where she learned of another vacancy.
- She applied without the required credential.
- She got the job first and then obtained the credential.

Convert Frustrations into Opportunities

Life rarely flows smoothly. It is rare for anyone to live for long without facing frustrations of some type. No one can win every time, and life would probably not be much fun if you could. The story of Karl illustrates that success is not in how much adversity you face, but in how you respond to it.

A Misfit Fits In

As a child, my parents decided it might be fun to bring up their kids speaking German. So my first language was German, which I, for years growing up, resented because I was in an Italian neighborhood. I just didn't feel as if I fit in.

In high school I was getting poor grades. I knew why and so did my parents. I was spending more time studying my fourteen-year-old girlfriend than my books. My parents broke us up and shipped me off to prep school. I was heartbroken.

Without the distraction, however, I started to work on my studies and was eventually admitted to one of the top universities in the United States. I tried out for the school newspaper but was turned down. I tried out for the drama club but never got called. These were two more big disappointments.

I then tried out for the college radio workshop, whose members wrote radio plays and presented them on local area radio stations. When I heard that a group was trying to start a college radio station, I finally got involved. I became the station's program director as a sophomore, its general manager as a junior.

After getting my degree in 1943, I wanted to join an officer's training program. However, the medical exam revealed a heart problem that classified me as 4F, unfit for military service. This was another great disappointment.

I decided to volunteer for the Office of War Information and learned there were current openings in London for people with radio experience and a knowledge of German (two qualifications I had not initially wanted).

Over the years a long series of other disappointments followed by unexpected successes have led me to my present position as the owner of three radio stations.

Note how Karl converted each frustration into a positive opportunity:
- He was frustrated about fitting into his neighborhood because he initially spoke German, but his German language ability was crucial in landing a key job.
- He was frustrated in losing his high school sweetheart, but he reacted by concentrating on his studies.
- He was frustrated in gaining admission to the school's newspaper staff and drama club, but he persisted by getting involved with the school's radio station.
- He was frustrated in his desire to join the military service because of his heart condition, but he found another way to contribute to the war effort.

Losing your job is more than frustrating — it can feel devastating. Suddenly your whole security blanket is jerked out from under you. You have no work, no security, no income and no status. Here is the story of how Francesca lost her security blanket and what she did about it.

A Truant Child Leads to a Great Job

I had been employed as a school counselor for just a year when the bad news hit. The school district was undergoing a severe budget crisis, and it had been decided that personnel cuts were necessary. Under the union contract those with the least seniority would be cut. I got the word that I was cut late at night, about 2:30 a.m. on a Friday. I was sick about being cut because I loved my work as a counselor and knew I had been making a big difference in the lives of my students.

To improve my future employability I enrolled in a program at the state university some fifty miles away. The program was designed to train teachers of emotionally impaired children. I also continued to "network" with friends and friends of friends. I approached a friend who worked at the County Office of Education and asked about options in the counseling field. There were none.

I continued to make periodic visits. Finally one day my friend informed me that a half-time truant officer position had been created and that they were looking for someone to fill it. I immediately applied for the job because I was desperate. I had absolutely no desire to be a truant officer, but it did have a reasonable salary attached. Because of my prior experience and current training I was given the appointment. It was only a half-time position, but I worked full time at it while at the same time carrying a full-time course load at the University.

In April of that year, late on an afternoon when I was supposed to be off duty, I went to visit administrators at the Eastern Elementary School about Rafael, a child who had been habitually truant from school. In the course of the discussion the Principal mentioned that they were creating a counselor position but had not yet made a formal job announcement. I jumped at the opportunity. Though my prior experience had been at the high school level, I knew that this was the chance I had been waiting for. I applied and was chosen for the job. It turned out to be the most satisfying job I had ever had. And it was all due to luck. If Rafael had not skipped school that day, I would never have known about the opportunity.

Was it really luck? Let's look at the actions Francesca took after she had been laid off from her high school job:

- She enrolled in a training program for teachers of emotionally impaired children.
- She kept in periodic contact with friends who might know about job openings.
- She accepted a half-time job as truant officer that she did not enjoy.
- She nevertheless worked full-time on the job.
- When she should have been off duty, she followed up on a child who was truant.
- She allowed the conversation with the Principal to veer onto topics other than one truant child.
- She expressed strong interest in the soon-to-be-opened position and got the job.

Francesca's persistent actions and hard work enabled her find the kind of job she wanted — even though she now attributes it all to luck.

Realize That Unplanned Events Result in More Unplanned Events

Francesca's story illustrates that multiple unplanned events may be combined before something better appears. Francesca had not planned to be laid off, to be a truant officer, to have Rafael skip school nor to find out about a future job opening.

Each event has multiple consequences — for you as well as for others. Each event sets the stage for subsequent events. No one can predict in advance how a string of unplanned events might affect anyone's career. John's story illustrates the effects of an unending sequence of interrelated but unpredictable events.

"Can I Major in Tennis, Coach?"

I grew up playing a variety of competitive games with my childhood friend, Alan, who lived in another part of our small Midwestern town. We started kindergarten together, then Alan changed schools and we lost contact for a while. We reconnected a few years later when I ventured into a new neighborhood on my bike, and happened to ride past his house while he was playing alone in the front yard. He taught me to play ping pong, and around age twelve we "graduated" from ping-pong in Alan's basement to tennis (borrowing his sister's new birthday gift rackets). We taught ourselves the game, and became skilled enough to play on our respective high school teams — sometimes in competition with each other.

We went to different colleges, where each of us made the varsity tennis team. My tennis team would travel to other colleges for team matches. Our coach, Dr. Wallar, and five players would ride together, leaving early on a Saturday morning, playing tennis all afternoon, enjoying a steak dinner, and returning home that evening. I got to know and like Dr. Wallar.

When I approached the end of my sophomore year in college, I received a letter from the Registrar's Office asking what my major would be. I had no idea and so threw the letter in the wastebasket. A month later I received a follow-up letter that I disposed of similarly. How was I supposed to choose a major? I had no idea. Finally I received the third letter which stated: "If you do not report to the Registrar's Office to declare a major by 5:00 p.m. on Friday, May 26, your registration will be terminated." "Hmmmm," I thought, "These guys are serious." But what was I to do? No one had ever offered any advice or instruction on how to choose a major. Maybe I ought to ask for help. But who could help me? The only faculty member I felt comfortable talking with was our tennis coach, Dr. Wallar, so I made an appointment to see him at 4:00 p.m. on Friday, May 26.

I should mention that at the small college I attended faculty members were often called upon to do double duty. Dr. Wallar was not only the tennis coach, he was the one and only professor of psychology. When I saw him, I wasted no time on polite chit-chat. "Dr. Wallar," I said, "Within the next hour I have to declare a major or my registration will be terminated. What do you think I should major in?" Quick as a wink he replied, "Psychology, of course." "OK, thanks," I called out over my shoulder as I dashed toward the door. I ran to the Registrar's office, arrived in plenty of time (thirty minutes to spare), wrote "psychology" on the appropriate form, signed my name and left the office with a sigh of relief. And that's how I started down the path toward becoming a psychologist. I feel infinitely lucky that all these unplanned events worked out so well. I stumbled into becoming a psychologist, and I'm convinced it has been the best possible career for me.

Let's think of the multiple unplanned events that influenced John's decision to major in psychology:

- There was no necessary reason why the tennis coach should also have been a professor of psychology. He might have been an economist, or a chemist, or a sociologist. Could that coincidence have affected John's career?
- Even though Dr. Wallar was a professor of psychology, he might not have recommended psychology as a major for John. He might have said, "You look like an English major to me." Would that response have affected John's career?
- Suppose Alan's sister had been given a bag of golf clubs instead of tennis rackets for her birthday. Would that gift have influenced John to take up golf instead of tennis?
- Suppose Alan had a photography lab instead of a ping-pong table in the basement. Would that difference in the availability of physical equipment have affected John's career?
- Suppose Alan had not been out in his front yard by himself when John cruised by on his bike. Would meeting someone other than Alan have affected the course of John's career?

No one can ever know what would have happened on the path not taken. But it seems reasonable to assume that John's career was significantly influenced by a whole host of unplanned events.

John's actions enabled these events to happen. Was John's career then totally due to these unplanned events? Was it just luck? Just an accident? What role did John himself play in creating his own career?

John was an active participant in all the events. Let's see exactly what John did:

- He went exploring on his bicycle.
- He stopped and chatted when he saw a familiar face.
- He agreed to play ping pong even though he didn't know how.
- He agreed to play tennis even though he didn't know how.
- He practiced and improved his tennis game.
- He volunteered for the varsity tennis teams in both high school and college.

- He finally asked for help in choosing a college major.
- He followed the advice he was given.
- Later, of course, John took many other constructive actions that enabled him eventually to become a psychologist (and to co-author this book).

Make the Job Fit You

There are ways to make almost any job more pleasant. Granted, it is sometimes easier to quit and find another job. However, it often pays to exert some effort in trying to modify the job or modify your approach to the job before giving up on it. Monique is a case in point.

Putting Myself in Charge

After getting a master's degree and knocking around Europe for four years, I decided it was time to go to work. I had no idea what I wanted to do. A former classmate asked if I'd like to be a consultant. I didn't know what that was, but I said yes. She gave me a number to call. I called, I visited the consulting firm. During the interview I ad-libbed answers to a dozen questions. I was offered a part-time temporary position. I wanted a full-time permanent position, but I said OK.

No one offered to teach me how to be a consultant. I invented everything I did. Four months later they gave me notice that I had been laid off. I requested a reversal. I won. Three years later, having worked nights, days and weekends supporting coworkers who did very little, I spun off as an "independent consultant" starting my own business. I am now in my twenty-fourth year of this improbable gig. I'm nationally known and solvent too!

Monique certainly took charge of her own life. She talked herself into a job she knew nothing about. She learned how to do it on her own. She overturned her lay-off notice. And she gained enough experience that she was able to launch her own consulting business. Monique did not fit the job. Monique made the job fit her.

As you try to make the most of unplanned events, remember these points:

- Take advantage of unexpected disappointments.
- Be open to changing locations and occupations.

- Share your interests and experiences with interesting people you meet.
- Convert frustrations into opportunities.
- Realize that unplanned events result in more unplanned events.
- Make the job fit you.

An Easy Exercise for Your Own Life

We have been telling you stories about other people, but you can learn most from applying these ideas to your own life. The following exercise is a starting point to get you thinking about your early aspirations and the unplanned events that have affected you. We want you to see that you are perfectly normal to have been influenced by unplanned events. We also want you to see that your own actions enabled unplanned events to happen and that your own actions capitalized on these events for your own benefit.

Your ideas about what you find satisfying continue to change throughout your life. Just as your childhood aspirations were not necessarily fulfilled, so your present plans may not necessarily lead you to what you want either. Unexpected events are happening all the time — often because of actions you are taking. Some of them can have a big impact on your career.

1. List three occupations to which you aspired at some time during your childhood.

    _____   _____

    _____

2. Have you ever actually been employed in any of these occupations?
    ___ Yes   ___ No

3. If "yes" to #2, how similar was the reality of the job to your childhood image of it?
    ___ Similar   ___ Somewhat different   ___Very different

4. What unexpected event contributed most to your getting your present (or most recent) employment?

    _____

    _____

5. What actions had you taken prior to that event that enabled you to be in a position to experience it?

_____

_____

6. What actions had you taken after the event that enabled you to take advantage of the opportunities it presented?

_____

_____

7. How satisfied are you with your present life?
   ___ Very satisfied
   ___ Partially satisfied
   ___ Dissatisfied

8. How might you adapt some of the actions that you took in questions 5 and 6 to begin moving you toward an even more satisfying life now?

_____

_____

_____

Making the Most of Happenstance

You have experienced some unplanned events in your life, and you've taken action to capitalize on at least one such experience. Now you know that you can create and benefit from unplanned events, and you're ready to learn how to apply this knowledge to whatever circumstances life brings you. The rest of this book will give you additional ideas and examples of how to do just that.

You'll also find in these pages that we contradict most of the common myths that you've probably heard about life- and career-planning. Consider these lists:

Common Myths About Planning Your Life and Career
- Don't let unexpected events disrupt your plans.
- Choose a career goal as soon as possible.
- Do all you can to make your "dream" come true.

- Take action only when you are sure of the outcome.
- Avoid making mistakes.
- Wait for a lucky break.
- Go for a job only if you have all the skills.
- Put your career first.
- Always hold on to your beliefs.
- Believe that luck is just an accident.

Just to let you anticipate how we will counter these myths, here is our actual advice in a nutshell, along with the chapters containing all the details.

Counter Myths

- Make the most of unplanned events. *(Review chapter 1.)*
- Always keep your options open. *(Read chapter 2.)*
- Wake up — before your "dream" comes true. *(Read chapter 3.)*
- Try it — even without knowing the outcome. *(Read chapter 4.)*
- Go ahead and make mistakes. *(Read chapter 5.)*
- Take action to create your own luck. *(Read chapter 6.)*
- Go for the job — then learn the skills. *(Read chapter 7.)*
- Enjoy yourself — the good life is a balanced life. *(Read chapter 8.)*
- Overcome self-sabotage. *(Read chapter 9.)*
- Remember that luck is no accident. *(Read chapter 10.)*

With the many options and action ideas you'll find in this book, you'll be ready to design your own game plan for making the most of happenstance in your life.

Chapter 2

Always Keep Your Options Open

When you come to a fork in the road, take it.
— Yogi Berra

The best way to predict the future is to create it.
— Peter Drucker

Everyone who got to where they are had to begin where they were.
— Richard Paul Evans

The question that I hate most that we ask of young people is, "What are you going to be when you grow up?" And the truth is, I still don't know at age 45.
— Michelle Obama

We have spent much of our lives helping people to make career decisions, but *we don't want you ever to make a career decision again*. Why? A "career decision" is usually interpreted as a permanent commitment to one occupation. But it is nonsense to commit to a single path when both you and the world you live in are constantly changing. We have now seen the error of our ways and consider ourselves to be "recovering" career counselors.

Instead of trying to decide your future today, you would be much better off keeping an open mind while actively exploring your opportunities. A single-minded focus on just one occupation produces "career tunnel vision."

In this chapter, we'll take a look at the dangers of narrowing your choice of careers too early. (The ideas we'll discuss in regard to careers, of course, may be applied to most important decisions about the direction of your life.)

Avoid Tunnel Vision

If you are like most people, as a child you probably tired of answering the question, "What are you going to be when you grow up?" Few children are precocious enough to respond, "An adult." The question assumes that a child can predict the future, ignoring the reality that even adults who are trained to predict the future (e.g., economists, stock brokers, meteorologists, political analysts) are frequently wrong. No one can predict the future accurately. There are too many unexpected events — too much happenstance — occurring every day.

In high school and college the pressure increases to get everyone to declare a future occupation. Some students sensibly and honestly refuse to commit to a single occupation, much to the dismay of their counselors, teachers and parents who then label these students as "undecided" or, even worse, "indecisive." The expectation is that you should commit to an occupation that you haven't even tried out yet.

FRANK & ERNEST By Bob Thaves

Reprinted with Permission of Newspaper Enterprise Association, Inc.

Tell others you're "open-minded" — not "undecided."

Adults who are laid off or are unemployed for any reason come under even more intense pressure to name a future occupation — now! We think that pressure can be destructive; you need time to create some options. If, as sometimes happens, you do need a job immediately, you can take the first job you find — whether you like it or not — while you search for other alternatives.

React to Pressure by Remaining Open-minded

When you were first asked, "What do you want to be when you grow up?" you probably felt forced to come up with an answer. Maybe you answered with something like firefighter, rock star, or basketball player. If you were to have answered the question with a response like "I don't know" or "How can you expect me to predict the future, I'm just a kid?!" you would have soon discovered that your answer was politically incorrect (even if it was actually the most sensible answer). People might even begin to wonder about you. Was your refusal to give a definitive answer a serious flaw in your character? Were you "flaky," or worst of all, "indecisive?" Much of career counseling has traditionally been all about helping you "cure" your indecision and state a clear career goal. We have no objection to tentative career goals combined with continual open-mindedness, but we hate to see people get trapped in an occupation that makes them miserable because their tunnel vision prevents them from seeing alternatives.

You Don't Need to Commit to a Future Goal

Let's think about how career choices are made. Did it ever seem crazy to you that you were expected to choose an occupation that you had never tried out? Not only choose it — but make a commitment to stick with it for the rest of your life! It's like asking you to choose your future spouse before the first date. Yet we live in a society where the normal expectation is that young people should be able to name their future occupations — and the sooner, the better.

Even Naming a Stopgap Occupation
May Cause Trouble Eventually

Coming up with a job title does get people off your back (albeit temporarily). If you are asked to name your future occupation and

Make decisions when the time is right.

you know it is politically incorrect to decline to answer, the easiest way out is to make up the name of some occupation. In fact, if you are especially aware of the political currents around you, you might get even more mileage out of your answer by naming an occupation assumed to be higher in prestige such as "doctor" or "lawyer." The tactic of naming a high prestige job does give you the temporary advantage of stopping people from bugging you with their questions, and it may gain you some hugs or pats on the back for being so ambitious. Of course, it takes no ambition at all to give a one-word answer to an absurd question, but you might as well take whatever credit you can get!

The trouble with naming any specific occupation in advance, although it may relieve the pressure temporarily, is that eventually you must take some action. If you had replied "lawyer," people will someday expect you to apply to law school, and you may feel committed to do so even though your original answer was designed just to get people off your back.

Many people find that the choices they made at one time in their lives are no longer relevant, but there is no need for anyone to feel guilty about this situation. You don't need to become trapped because of one early choice. You have many options.

Liberate Yourself from Unrealistic Expectations

You might be interested to learn why we now feel the way we do about career "planning." We came to the realization that our own careers were a matter of creating and capitalizing on *unexpected opportunities*. Then in surveying numerous adult populations we discovered that only about *2 percent* of the people claim to be working now in the occupation they had planned when they were eighteen years old. The goal of naming a future occupation seemed to be an exercise in futility. Goals are influenced by thousands of unplanned events for everyone.

Let us tell you a bit of our own history. We feel liberated by the realization that we don't need to plan an unforeseeable future, and we want you to feel liberated too.

Why John Krumboltz Abandoned a Lucrative Career as a Professional Baseball Player

When I was thirteen years old growing up in Cedar Rapids, Iowa, I had already decided I would become a professional baseball player. My father and I would attend baseball games of the Cedar Rapids Raiders, and I knew the record of each player on the team. I played in the equivalent of what is now called "Little League," and I fancied myself as quite a good baseball player. I could catch fly balls, pick up grounders and place my hits with considerable agility.

Then one day my career plans changed drastically. Our team was playing another team whose pitcher was a tall, strong, lanky sixteen-year old named "Lefty." (Several years later I was told that Lefty was pitching for the Cleveland Indians.) On that day none of the players on our team was able to get on base against Lefty. Then my turn at bat came up. I was sure

I could get a hit. I swaggered up to the plate swinging my bat in what I hoped would be perceived as a menacing manner. I took my position in the batters box and awaited the first pitch. Lefty went into his windup and threw his first pitch. The ball was headed straight at my head at ninety miles an hour! I dove into the dirt to escape and looked up just in time to see the ball curve right over the middle of the plate for a called strike.

At that instant my plans to become a professional baseball player changed. How was I to know that the pitch was going to curve over the plate? What if it had been a fast ball on a straight line toward my head? I would have been killed. I valued my life too much to risk it on the gamble of whether the ball would curve or not. No sir! Not for me! I didn't know what else I could do, but I was not going to become a professional baseball player.

In the years since that fateful day I have wondered about my career planning thought process.
- I thought I was a pretty good ball player.
- I thought it would be fun to play baseball and get paid for it too.
- I allowed one pitch to change my plans.
- I might have learned how to distinguish curve balls from fast balls.
- But, I might have been killed during the learning process.

"In retrospect," John sums up, "I'm glad I gave up my dream. I never had the makings of a professional baseball player. If I had not learned my baseball shortcomings at age thirteen, I'm sure I would have learned them soon after, perhaps in some other way." (As you learned in chapter 1, John soon after discovered tennis, a "safer" sport that had a lasting impact on his career and his life.)

The experience illustrates how small learning experiences can have major impacts on career and life plans and how quickly plans can change in the light of unexpected events.

How Al Levin Benefited from Bad Advice

Ever since I could remember, I thought I would be a lawyer. My parents planted the idea in my head at a very early age. I guess they thought that was a high prestige and secure career option. The first time I remember answering the what-are-you-going-to-be-when-you-grow-up question, I remember answering "a star running back with the LSU Tigers." My answer was based on watching a college football game on television and loving the LSU uniforms. But I still knew that I would probably end up as a lawyer. I never became either one. I hated football practice years later in high school because it was so regimented, and I failed to study for the LSAT and probably had the lowest score possible. Another major problem that I didn't realize at the time concerned the fact that I had no idea of what a lawyer really did.

I ended up (after graduating from college) jumping from one job to another, including a stint as a copy machine repair man (I took the job because I was able to have a company car), a substitute teacher (getting punched in the arm by a first grader and getting an orange thrown at my head in a high school), and a telephone book delivery man (on curvy Lombard Street in San Francisco, no less).

It wasn't until I was in my late twenties that I realized that I needed some help sorting out my career plans. I remember meeting with a career counselor at my university career center. She took one quick glance at my resume, handed me a list of prospective employers and sent me on my way. So much for dedicated service to alumni! Anyway, this meeting with a career counselor unexpectedly changed my life forever. I realized that you could actually earn a decent living (on a college campus no less), listening to a few questions, handing someone a piece of paper, and then sending the person on his or her way!

Seriously, for a while I became a career counselor because my experience with a career counselor was so bad. Here I was, an educated young man seeking a little help, and getting none. I was feeling that my education was a waste and I was a total failure. I needed real help, and didn't get any. I was sure that I could learn how to do a better job of career counseling than the counselor I experienced. I entered a graduate program in counseling and dedicated myself to really helping people with career problems. Now I am educating future career counselors as a faculty member at California State University, Sacramento and doing my best to provide better advice than I had received.

In the words of a recent wise high school graduate, when you make future plans, you better "write in pencil and have an eraser ready."

Respond Positively to Challenging Questions

As you can tell from our stories, our careers turned out very differently than we had originally planned. Let's consider some illustrative questions you might have if and when you succumb to the pressure of naming a future occupational goal.

"Do I Really Have to Do What I Said I Would Do?"

No, you don't. Other people begin to put pressure on you to behave in ways you may not want. If you declared as a child you wanted to be a doctor because you got a pat on the back, your parents may have given you a laboratory kit as a birthday present and prodded you to join the Science Club in school. Their actions were well intentioned and might even have been beneficial, but their expectations put pressure on you to move in one particular direction when your original declaration may have been fleeting and now no longer have any real meaning for you.

The real trouble comes when you begin to feel obliged to do something. You wake up one morning and realize that eventually you have to take some action — get a job, join the Army, go to college. If you go to college, further actions will be necessary later. We admit that there is a certain security in having named a future occupation. People then guide you toward certain academic majors and training programs (even though your original choice was only supposed to get them off your back.) But then if you are not careful, you find that you are graduating from school and people actually expect you to work in an occupation for which you trained.

"What If I Don't Like the Field for Which I Trained?"

You can do something else. But you are thinking: "I have made this tremendous investment of time, money and energy, and now I don't like it?! How ungrateful! How wasteful!" Shame on you, they (and you) might think. You will feel guilty and feel a sense of obligation to continue working in this occupation that you now find so distasteful.

But it is nonsense to continue working in a job that you hate. You have the rest of your life ahead of you. Why should you suffer for the rest of your life because of a decision you made years ago?! You can learn how to change. That's what this book is all about.

"But Isn't It Good to Make Future Plans?"

Not if you feel trapped by them. You may believe that you should know what your lifetime goals are and that you should have a plan for achieving them. We disagree. We have all been led to believe that planning is the answer. We are not against planning itself — we are against sticking with plans that prove unsatisfactory.

Blondie By Young & Lebrun

Feel free to change direction at any time in your life.

"Do I Want to Rely on Chance Events?"

You can rely on unpredictable events playing a role in your career, but that does not mean you lose control. On the contrary, you can create chance events that may be beneficial, and you can learn to take advantage of opportunities that arise from them. You never need to be ashamed of the part that chance plays. Chance events open up opportunities that you never could have anticipated. Everyone's career is affected by chance events. This book is about ways to create and capitalize on chance events and we are going to give you many examples.

Refuse to Serve a Life Sentence of Misery

Many people find that the choices they made at one time in their lives are no longer relevant, but there is no need for anyone to feel guilty about this situation. You don't need to serve a life sentence of misery because of one early career choice. You have many options. This book is designed to help you explore numerous options and take actions that will enable you to create a more satisfying life for yourself.

In this chapter, we've advocated that you always keep your options open and that you can

- avoid tunnel vision;
- react to pressure by remaining open-minded;
- liberate yourself from unrealistic expectations;
- respond positively to challenging questions;
- refuse to serve a life sentence of misery.

Keeping Your Options Open — an Exercise

It can seem scary at first, this idea that you don't choose a single path and follow it. As you've seen, however, life usually doesn't work that way anyway! So why not prepare yourself for the "real world" by keeping your options open?

As you look at the items below, consider how this self-exploration exercise might help you to be more open to the possibilities.

1. Have you ever felt pressure to name a career goal?
   ____ Yes
   ____ No

2. If "Yes," what kind of goal did you feel you were supposed to choose? _____

   _____

3. How did you react to this pressure?
   ____ a. I named a career that satisfied others.
   ____ b. I named a career that satisfied me.
   ____ c. I refused to name any career.
   ____ d. Other (Specify):

   _____

4. How will you react to requests to specify your future plans the next time you are asked?
   ____ a. I'll say I'm not ready to answer yet.
   ____ b. I'll describe the actions I'm taking to come up with a good answer.
   ____ c. I'll just name the first field that comes into my mind.
   ____ d. I'll name the career that they want to hear.
   ____ e. I'll tell them that I don't make future plans.
   ____ f. Other (Specify):

   _____

5. If you have spent years training for a career you no longer enjoy, can you dare to consider other possibilities — a career change?

   _____

   _____

6. What steps would you have to take to open up a new career for yourself? _____

   _____

   _____

7. What's stopping you? _____

   _____

   _____

Making the Most of Happenstance

Chances are you have been given tons of advice about your future by family members, friends, teachers, counselors or religious leaders. This book offers you a chance to examine a few common beliefs and see which ones have influenced your thinking. We are advocating a radical shift away from these ideas that are commonly accepted. We would like you to think through your own assumptions. Which of these ideas have you heard? Are you ready to make the most of unexpected events in your life? Will you dare to keep your options open? Read on!

Chapter 3

Wake Up — Before Your Dream Comes True!

The first step in making your dreams come true is to wake up.
— Paul Valery

Do not dwell in the past, do not dream of the future, concentrate the mind on the present moment.
— Buddha

You need a big dream and little steps.
— Diane Von Furstenberg

Dreams can help you create a vision of your future career. Perhaps you have a dream of the career you want. Maybe you want to lead a rock band, become president of the United States, or be the scientist who discovers the cure for cancer. If your dream inspires you to try new activities, we encourage you to continue to dream about the future — and take action to make it happen.

Some people believe that a career must be based on discovering your dream or passion. Once that passion is uncovered, they believe, the rest will take care of itself. Perhaps one reason this notion is so captivating is because our belief in dreams is deeply rooted in the most ancient cultural, historical and literary myths.

Striving to fulfill one's dream is part of our cultural heritage. The Declaration of Independence asserted that the pursuit of happiness was one of our unalienable rights, and we are frequently advised to "Live the American dream." The contents of that dream are never too clear — though the suggestion usually implies a prestigious job, a house in the suburbs, a happy marriage and two perfect children.

We all love to believe that our dreams will come true, to read romantic stories with happy endings. But what if the ending is not happy? What if the dream becomes a nightmare? Most of us naively expect our dreams will be fulfilled. Emotional devastation can be the consequence when they are not. What if you apply to your dream college and you are not admitted? What if you accept a dream job and find that the boss is an ogre? What if you build your dream house and the neighbors turn out to be trashy? How will you handle the situation? We generally receive no instruction in how to react to the failure of our dreams.

Our purpose in this chapter — and in this book — is to prepare you to deal with real life. Dreams are wonderful, and we urge you to go ahead and enjoy your dream and try to make it happen. Don't be surprised, however, if the dream does not work out exactly as you planned. Some unforeseen event may change your life — for better or for worse. Some people have found out that waking up from a dream was the best thing that could have happened. We would never discourage you from pursuing your dream, but we would advise you to keep your eyes and ears open along the way. Unplanned events can lead to even better outcomes if you are ready to seize opportunities when they arise.

When Dreams Fail, Move on to Something Else

OK. Unfortunate, but true: reality does not always conform to our dreams. How do you deal with that? Here's one real-world approach: *experiment with your dreams*. Try them out. See how it goes. Do your best, then evaluate the results. You're bound to learn some valuable lessons even if things don't work out the way you hoped. Let's take a look at some examples.

Chitra's experience illustrates that your dream may not turn out as you had imagined but that alternatives learned along the way may lead to more satisfying opportunities.

Talking with a Gorilla

My dream and passion was to work in the field of ape sign language studies. It was indeed true that my dream and passion gave me (an English major with teaching experience but with no prior background in primatology, anthropology, psychology, zoology, or linguistics) the courage, energy, will and chutzpah to sign up for primatology courses, get A's in all of them, and apply for a job in an obviously limited field. In fact, I did get my dream job working on ape language studies with a signing gorilla, but I soon quit this "dream" job, heartbroken by the politics of working in an isolated, dysfunctional environment, and disenchanted with the lack of research conducted.

My dream job was shattered, but I never gave up the dream that I could be happy. I then tried a number of jobs — teaching again, working in a hospital, working for a nonprofit organization. Nothing seemed right. I contacted several career counselors and explained my fear of making another mistake as I contemplated getting a Master's degree in counseling psychology. One counselor told me something that revolutionized my life and my thinking. He simply said, "Chitra, you've got to make mistakes; it's OK to make mistakes; it's good to make mistakes; that's the only way to learn." That statement liberated me from my fear. Maybe getting that Master's degree would be a mistake, maybe it wouldn't. So what? I'd learn something along the way, and I'd approach the experience as an adventure. Immediately after that conversation I filled out my application to graduate school and sent it in.

I was admitted, went to school full-time, worked part-time and completed three internships in two years. I learned that what I enjoyed most was talking with people about their passions. Now I am working as a career counselor helping welfare mothers find satisfying employment. I am touched by their stories and am experimenting with new ways of helping them. My life is very meaningful and fulfilling, and yet at the same time I am presented with new opportunities for growth and development. Currently I am hoping to go on to get a Ph.D. — and I don't care whether that's a mistake or not!

Chitra started with the belief that there was one dream job out there that would be perfect for her if she could just find it. That belief is dangerous in itself, since no job is perfect; every job has its moments of drudgery along with its moments of exhilaration.

Note the actions Chitra took to advance her career:
- She tried English teaching but didn't like it.
- She took all the courses needed to work in ape sign language learning.
- She applied for and obtained her "dream job."
- When the dream job proved to be more of a nightmare job, she quit.
- She experimented with other jobs, none of which satisfied her.
- She shared with a career counselor her fear of making another mistake.
- When the counselor gave her "permission" to make mistakes, she applied for graduate school.
- She worked hard to make her graduate school experience a good one.
- She found a job that enabled her to engage in satisfying tasks much of the time.
- She applied for doctoral level study.

In her own words, Chitra is no longer troubled with the fear of making a career mistake.

Deciding Is Easy — Making It Happen Is the Hard Part

Nikki's story does not have such a happy ending. Here is how she pursued her dream job.

On Becoming a Doctor

I had majored in English and journalism. After several years as a newspaper reporter I was promoted to editor. People told me that I was creative and talented in my editing work, but something was missing for me. I went to a career counselor who asked about my dream job. I confided that my lifelong dream was becoming a doctor. He said, "If that is your dream, go for it."

I decided I would abandon my newspaper editorship and become a doctor. I told everyone about my decision. I was so happy and proud to have decided to be a doctor. I started taking all the requisite courses needed for a medical school application. I had no idea how difficult those basic physics and mathematics courses would be. I flunked them. I was forced to give up my "dream," and the ensuing depression and self-doubt still plague me.

I moved to another part of the country and returned to my editorial work. I am now editing web sites for a start-up company.

Reprinted with Permission of United Feature Syndicate, Inc.

Try taking small steps before jumping to a conclusion

Nikki cannot be blamed for pursuing her dream. Her counselor gave her the green light, but there were many other factors that needed to be considered. The counselor might better have advised her along these lines: "Nikki, before you throw yourself into the deep end of the pool, why don't you stick your big toe into the water first? Find out what courses are required for admission to medical school. Take one of them at night at the community college. See how it goes for you. Then we can talk about next steps."

A decision to become a doctor is only the first small step in the long process of actually becoming a doctor. Nikki was proud of her decision to become a doctor, but she really had not considered all the hurdles she still had to jump just to get into medical school. Had she asked for our advice, we would have been tempted to respond along these lines: "Nikki, come on now, get real. In a split second anyone can decide to become a doctor. *Deciding is easy. Making it happen is the hard part.* Don't brag to your friends that you have decided to become a doctor. You have nothing to brag about yet. Tell your friends that you are exploring career possibilities. Tell them that you are finding out more about what is required in fields you're interested in. Tell them that you are taking a course in night school and that you'll see how that goes before taking the next step."

As author, humorist, and radio personality Garrison Keillor put it, "Some luck lies in not getting what you thought you wanted but getting what you have, which once you have got it you may be smart enough to see is what you would have wanted had you known."

Test Your Dream — One Step at a Time

Nikki's mistake was to jump into a new career commitment virtually sight unseen. While such impetuous behavior may occasionally work out, we think you are better advised to proceed in gradual steps. As an illustration, consider Herb's story.

From Stockbroker to Singer

Herb enjoyed music and dreamed of becoming a singer. He began singing as a child, and music became a serious hobby. His father, a successful investment banker, persuaded Herb to go into business as a stockbroker. Herb was quite successful in selling stocks. All during his career in finance, however, he was singing at the parties and weddings of friends.

Although Herb was not getting much personal satisfaction from his work in banking, he found it difficult to give up the benefits of a successful business career. He was able to gradually increase the number of singing invitations he accepted, and soon was having the time of his life after work hours — as the lead singer in a rock band. Herb didn't want to burn his bridges, however: "I got a real sense of security from having money flow in from my singing while I was still a stockbroker."

He obtained a three-month leave of absence (unpaid) from his firm and used the time to polish his singing style, with the help of a talented voice coach. He kept in touch with his Wall Street contacts, in case the musical career did not work out as he hoped. Luck and talent worked for him, however, and he didn't need his backup plan. His group became one of the top rock bands in the Chicago area, recorded some successful CDs, and toured throughout the Midwest. The last we heard, he had no plans to return to the world of finance.

Herb had not jumped suddenly from stockbroker to singer. His transition involved a gradual evolution over time in which he began spending increasing amounts of time doing what he enjoyed most. He did not burn his bridges. Let's check the steps:

- He began singing as a child.
- His talents as a musician were recognized by family and friends.
- His father insisted the music must remain just a hobby while business took priority.
- He continued to perform musically while still employed as a stockbroker.
- He took a leave of absence (he did NOT quit) to concentrate on his music.
- He saw that his part-time singing was earning money.
- He became a full-time singer and has not needed to cross back on his bridge.

Don't Stick with a Bad Choice

It is common for people to succumb to the demands of family, school, or society that an occupational goal be declared in advance. Sometimes the choice works out satisfactorily. At other times great unhappiness ensues. When the choice turns out to be a bad one, it's dangerous to assume that you must continue. Sometimes persistence at a difficult task is the best course of action, but when the task itself is distasteful, it is perfectly legitimate to consider making a change. It might be nice if there were clear cut rules: "Keep persisting until you finally get what you want" OR "Quit and try something else the first time you run into difficulty." But neither of these rules makes sense. People who find themselves in difficulty may be trying to apply either one of these rules. The case of Lorraine illustrates the anxiety generated by the belief that you must persist at a distasteful activity simply because you started it.

"Listening to My Gut"

In my family, I learned there were two primary career trajectories: trading futures on the Mercantile Exchange or becoming a lawyer. I chose the latter because it sounded more interesting to spend my day reading case law, writing, and doing research rather than shouting numbers and making hand signals in a trading pit. Within the first year, however, I became disenchanted with my graduate program and the law profession. I found most of the case studies to be very dry and the competition among students to be fierce. Taking a part-time position as a clerk in a small law firm confirmed what I already knew in my gut — this work was not for me.

Although I was miserable, I thought that perhaps there were legitimate reasons to finish law school. After all, I was almost a third of the way through the program. I heard that the first year was the hardest. I decided to take an informal poll among my first-year classmates. I asked them what made them decide to go to law school. The vast majority replied that they didn't know what else to do with their lives and that this path, incidentally, made their parents quite happy.

That response was not enough justification to put myself through at least two more years of misery. After a few more months of heavy soul searching, I defected from my graduate program. Unfortunately, I found that leaving wasn't that easy. Not only did I have to contend with my own confusion and guilt for not completing something I had started, I also had to deal with other people's reactions to my decision. When several close friends and family members asked, "So, what are you going to do now?" — as if I should have already reached closure on my career plans — I froze. The truth was that I had no idea how to respond to that question. I was not only integrating the loss of leaving law school, but also the loss of the dream that I had envisioned for my adult life.

Unlike my law school classmates who had temporarily chosen to dodge the sixty-four million dollar question of what they would do with the rest of their adult lives, by leaving my graduate program I had to wrestle with this question head on. The more I tried to force an answer, the more elusive it became. I was lost in a sea of anxiety and confusion. No one told me that it was normal for a "twenty something" not to know what she wanted to do. Nor did anyone suggest that I might use this time wisely by giving myself permission to explore other things.

Partly as a way to escape my anxiety about not knowing what I wanted to do, I found myself gravitating toward work that I had done as a volunteer during college — providing basic counseling and education services for women in a family planning setting. I secured such a position, and in many ways, it was a much better fit for me than law school. I felt more camaraderie among the staff and also enjoyed the work content. After several years, however, I found myself becoming intellectually bored and restless. I toyed with the idea of a graduate program in counseling but hesitated because I feared dropping out as I had done earlier in law school.

I made two destructive assumptions here: (1) if I dropped out once, that would make me more vulnerable to dropping out a second time, and (2) if I dropped out a second time that would mean I was a failure at graduate studies, and perhaps even a failure at work. In effect, I front-loaded the stakes. On the other hand, if I stayed where I was, I thought I would eventually die of boredom.

I decided to contact an advisor in the graduate counseling program at San Francisco State University. I relayed some of my past experience and she suggested that I give myself an opportunity to test the waters by enrolling as an unclassified student. That suggestion was all I needed. That spring, I signed up for courses in developmental foundations and career counseling. Being in graduate school made me realize how much I had been starving for intellectual stimulation. I soaked the material up like a sponge.

The instructor in my developmental foundations course invited the associate director of a local University's Career Center as a guest speaker during one of our classes. My full attention was riveted on the associate director while she conducted a mock career counseling role play. I thought to myself, "This role play was fascinating. I wish I had received some career counseling years ago when I was contemplating my own decision to attend law school. Perhaps I would have gone down an entirely different career path if I had received appropriate intervention." A moot thought at this point.

After class, I introduced myself to our guest speaker and asked her how I could find out more information about this kind of work. She suggested that I meet her at the Career Center for an "information interview." At the time, I didn't have the foggiest idea what an "information interview" was. All I knew was that I was very excited to learn about a whole new field.

I asked many questions about the work. The associate director was very friendly and forthcoming with answers. At the end of our scheduled meeting, I asked her what would be appropriate next steps. She suggested that I consider working as a volunteer for the Center during that following summer. I didn't have to think about my decision very long. I definitely wanted to try this out. I spent the summer helping out at the front desk, observing career counseling staff work with students and learning about resource materials. By the end of the summer, I was already hooked.

I declared career counseling as my major in graduate school, and I obtained a year-long internship. I was thrilled. And to think that I had had no previous plans whatsoever to go into this work.

After I finished my internship, I stayed in close contact with my supervisor. Three years later she called to say that another university was looking for a part-time career consultant. I applied, got the job and have expanded my role to provide trainings and workshops for the professional staff and supervise a graduate intern. How ironic to be training professional staff and supervising a graduate counseling intern, when only a short time ago, I had no clear idea about what I wanted to do!

The twists and turns in Lorraine's career which led her to find a satisfying set of work tasks started from her originally making a poor occupational choice. She did make a career decision — not wisely perhaps, and not from a very long list of alternatives. She gave it a good try — one year in law school. Note then the series of actions she initiated:

- She polled her classmates about their reasons for attending law school.
- She resigned from law school.
- She obtained counseling work in a family planning center.
- She asked for advice from a graduate advisor.
- She enrolled in graduate level courses just to try them out.
- She introduced herself to a guest speaker.
- She conducted an information interview.
- She volunteered to work one summer at the Career Center.

- She obtained a year's internship.
- She maintained a good relationship with her supervisor.
- She applied for and obtained a job as a career consultant.

She took all these actions to rescue herself from a career choice that she had believed she was supposed to stick with throughout her life. She was feeling guilt about violating the rule that she should persist indefinitely. She needed someone to tell her it was okay to try something else, someone to tell her that there is no such persistence rule. She suffered emotionally from her belief at first, but eventually took actions that freed her to create a more satisfying life.

ZITS By Jerry Scott and Jim Borgman

© Zits Partnership. Reprinted with Special Permission of King Features Syndicate

Reduce stress by recognizing you can't plan your whole life in advance.

Listen to Advice, But Make Up Your Own Mind

In some cultures it is traditional for parents to prescribe the career path their children should take. Even in the United States, some parents have a career dream for their children. The problem is that the children can feel obligated to live out the dream, even if it's not their own. When that happens, it can be a formula for unhappiness.

My Son, the Computer Engineer

Tai and Xaolu had immigrated to the United States from Taiwan. America was truly the land of opportunity for the young couple, and through hard work and long hours, they were able to save some money and start a small business all their own. When their son Edward was born, Tai and Xaolu couldn't have been happier. Their dream of coming to a new country, starting a successful business, and raising a family was coming true.

Edward was a very talented little boy, excelling in school at an early age. He maintained excellent grades throughout his schooling and was admitted to a prestigious university. His parents began to dream of the future that Edward could have in the country that had given them the opportunity to realize their dreams.

The "hot" career fields were computers and engineering. Every time Edward came home for a visit or they spoke to their son on the phone, Tai and Xaolu said how wonderful it would be if Edward were to pursue engineering.

There was only one problem: Edward didn't enjoy engineering. He had many diverse interests, including literature, history, and psychology but, unfortunately, engineering was not among them. Nevertheless, he decided to "bite the bullet" and took the prerequisites in engineering. For the first time in his life, Edward's grades began to fall. When he came home during a semester break, his parents were devastated with his "failure." (Anything less than an "A" was deemed a failure in his family!) For the first time in his life Edward told his parents that he hated school.

Fortunately, there's a happy ending to the story. With help from his university counselor, Edward was able to learn negotiation skills and was able to convince his parents that other career options were more aligned with his needs. Unfortunately, Edward is probably the exception in these situations.

Cultures differ in the extent to which parents have the power to influence the career paths of their children. In the mainstream

American culture, parents tend to be cautious about attempting to impose their career views on their children. The familiar saying is, "You can do anything you want to do." In other cultures parents are expected to influence their children's occupational pursuits. The judgment may be based on what is best for the family, not necessarily what is best for the child. Our individualistic American values lead us to express caution about creating a dream scenario for someone else who may not share the same dream.

Reassess Priorities as Circumstances Change

Your dream may conform well with reality — at first. However, with the economy, natural disasters, accidents, politics and illnesses, conditions change and can make an initial plan no longer satisfactory.

Sometimes you can achieve your dream career. That doesn't mean that the dream can last forever. The case of Isabel illustrates this point.

"If You Want God to Laugh..."

I knew I wanted to be a human resources director since the ninth grade. As early as the tenth grade I acted on my dream by becoming the personnel manager of my junior achievement business club. At the age of twenty-five I achieved my career goal and became a human resources director. I continued on this path and made a six figure income as an international human resources manager at age thirty. At the age of thirty-two, I discovered I had a bone tumor in the middle of my face and it could be cancerous. Since you can't excise a face like you can an arm or breast, the odds of survival were about fifty percent. After four surgeries, seeing more than thirty-five health care professionals, trying fifteen alternative therapies, it was declared that I had permanent nerve damage to my face and the prognosis was a lifetime of burning pain.

I realized that I had to give up my dream job because of the intensity that it demanded. I needed to find a job with less stress to help keep better control of the pain. While this was happening, my company was in the midst of layoffs. With the assistance of an outplacement firm, I began to reassess my priorities. The outplacement counselor helped me to consider other options. I quit and I am now working part-time as an HR consultant. I can truly understand what it feels like to be plucked out of your life for no apparent reason and have it changed forever. The tumor taught me that you can't control or predict life. It's just like a saying I once heard: "If you want God to laugh, tell Him your future plans."

Dreams can give people the impetus to pursue remarkable paths and adventures, and to be bold and brave visionaries. At the same time, dreams do not always come true. Even jobs which seem initially satisfying may not last forever. Interests change, priorities change, and circumstances change. As Isabel's story demonstrates, life may present conditions beyond our control. Are you prepared to adjust?

Passions are Created by Taking Action

A common illusion holds that job satisfaction comes from identifying a hidden passion and making the one right occupational choice early in life. We see that passion does not necessarily precede action — it may be created later as a result of your actions.

Passion for a line of work is often generated through significant interactions with other people. The story of Polly Matzinger illustrates how you can initiate such interactions.

Don't Be Afraid to Ask Questions

"I dropped in and out of college for years," recalls Polly Matzinger. She had worked as a jazz musician, carpenter, waitress, dog trainer, and even a Playboy bunny. "I decided that every job was boring and that I'd be a cocktail waitress and train dogs all my life." One night while eavesdropping on a conversation at the bar among a group of faculty members from the local university, she couldn't resist asking a question about evolutionary adaptations in skunks. One of the professors who ran the university's wildlife program was intrigued by her question. "He went on a campaign. He'd bring me articles and say, 'Read this,' and then come back and discuss them."

With the professor's help, Polly enrolled at the University of California at San Diego to pursue a Ph.D. in science. "What's nice about science," Polly says, "is that if things don't make sense, you can question them and not get fired for it."

"She's Not Afraid To Ask Questions," by Michael Ryan, *Parade Magazine*, March 24, 2002, page 12. Reprinted by permission.

Dr. Matzinger's story doesn't end there. She has created a new passion from her work. It concerns her theory about the immune system. Some researchers believe that it may revolutionize the way we treat cancer and other diseases. Let's look at the actions that she took to create her passion:

- She was intrigued by a conversation among a group of faculty from the local university and asked them a question.
- She made friends with one of the faculty members.
- She read and discussed articles about science that he brought to her.
- She took his advice and encouragement and applied for graduate school.
- She worked hard and completed a Ph.D.
- She created a theory about the immune system that may some day cure cancer.

Don't "Marry" an Occupational Goal

The common wisdom is that you should decide on an occupation so that you have a definite goal to guide your efforts. Sometimes that works out fine, but you need to avoid tunnel vision in your pursuit of a single occupational goal. Sometimes other opportunities arise.

Don't automatically reject opportunities because they do not fit your predetermined goal. They might be opportunities that you would enjoy even more than the one you originally chose. They may also provide you with the prerequisite experience you need to qualify for the goal you want. Erica's case illustrates the dangers of tunnel vision.

"I Stuck with My Goal — Now I'm Stuck"

When I moved to Dallas, I took a job part-time at an aerobics studio so that I could work out for free while I looked for the one kind of job I really wanted — being an art director for an advertising agency. At the aerobics studio I met a girl who worked for a shoe manufacturer. She helped me get in as a freelancer there to design graphics for the bottoms of shoes. (I had never realized that someone had to design the bottoms of shoes!)

The head shoe designer liked me so much that she offered me a position to design shoes. It was a good job — it made use of my artistic inclinations and it paid well. However, I had told everyone that I was going to get a job as an art director for an advertising agency, and so, unfortunately, as it turned out, I declined the offer.

I was afraid to take the risk of departing from my stated goal even though I did not have any offers for work in that area. I've had other offers to do display work and to work for internet companies, but I have been afraid to say yes to something I don't know. I feel that my career has stagnated because I am afraid to take a risk and do something other than what I initially declared. I am still unemployed.

Erica did take some constructive actions:
- She took a part-time job at an aerobics studio.
- She talked with people there.
- She accepted a free-lance designing job.

But then she made some decisions that she now regrets:
- Having told people she wanted to be an art director (an occupation for which she had no prerequisite experience), she declined job offers that would have given her that experience.
- She was afraid to accept jobs because she didn't already know how to do them.
- She refused to take risks.

Open Yourself to Other Alternatives

The personal stories in this chapter contain an important lesson. You may be so intent on achieving one particular dream that you ignore or reject other opportunities that arise during the pursuit. We don't know all of the opportunities the people in our stories encountered, and we'll never know what would have ensued had they taken another path. However, the single-minded focus on one objective, while it may pay off for some people, often blocks us from seeing and capitalizing on unexpected opportunities.

The whole notion that careers can and should be planned in advance is an unrealistic dream. Many people suffer from the myth that their future career path can be foretold. They are often overwhelmed by anxiety because they think they must find the "one right job" and that there is some way to know in advance what it should be. In their understandable but impossible striving for career certainty, they make themselves miserable.

Stuart Conger, former director of National Career Services in Canada, stated it this way:

"I wonder if our belief in occupational goals is falsely placed . . . Better to focus on 'making your job everything that it can be' rather than trying to identify the one occupation that will be best for you."

People who are unable to realize their dreams are understandably disillusioned by their experiences. If you make a major emotional investment in achieving one particular outcome, the failure to achieve the dream can be devastating. However, there is another way to pursue a dream without feeling destroyed if it fails to materialize: *Take an experimental attitude*. Instead of saying to yourself, "I must become a doctor," try saying, "I want to explore a career in medicine. I'll give it my best shot to see if I can get into medical school. If I get any better ideas along the way, I'll stay flexible." Or, instead of saying, "My dream is gone," try saying, "Now that things have changed, how can I begin to explore new opportunities that may be better for me?" Changing your plans is not failure. Changing your plans is perfectly normal. As you learn more, you may discover that your original dream no longer suits you. There are other experiments you will want to try next. We know one elderly gentleman who still says, "I haven't decided what I'm going to be when I grow up." Some of us think all of life is one continuous experiment!

How to Wake Up from Your Dream

So go ahead and dream, but keep yourself awake by remembering these points:

- When dreams fail, move on to something else.
- Test your dream one step at a time.
- Don't stick with a bad choice.
- Listen to advice, make up your own mind.
- Reassess priorities when circumstances change.
- Create passion by taking action.
- Don't "marry" an occupational goal.
- Open yourself to other alternatives.

A "Dream Work" Exercise

The following questions are designed to help you consider your own past and present "dream jobs" and evaluate your approach to the options that may be available to you.

1. What was one "dream job" that never materialized for you?

   _____

   _____

2. What convinced you that your dream was not to happen?

   _____

   _____

3. What action did you take when your dream failed to materialize in the way you had hoped?

   _____

   _____

4. What "dream job" do you have in mind right now?

   _____

   _____

5. You can have more than one dream. What other dream jobs have you thought about?

   _____

   _____

6. If you were serious about pursuing a dream job, what would be the first step you could take today?

   _____

   _____

7. How do circumstances differ now from those that led you to your present position?

   _____

   _____

8. Given today's circumstances, what choices would you like to make?

   _____

   _____

9. Do you feel stuck now with a bad choice you made in the past?
   Yes ___   No ___

10. If "Yes," what can you do now to get unstuck?
    _____
    _____

11. What advice have you received from others?
    _____
    _____

12. How are you reacting to that advice?
    ___ I tend to accept it uncritically
    ___ I tend to react defensively
    ___ I take it into account as I make my own plans
    ___ (other) _____

13. What steps could you take to transform your present job into one that would be more satisfying for you?
    _____
    _____

14. What keeps you from trying your other dreams?
    _____
    _____

Making the Most of Happenstance

We don't want you to stop dreaming. We want you to know that your dreams may change as you test them out. Your reality might be even better than your dreams — especially if you are willing to try out new adventures with unknown outcomes.

Chapter 4

Try It — Even Without Knowing the Outcome

You may be disappointed if you fail, but you are doomed if you don't try.
— Beverly Sills

Only those who will risk going too far can possibly find out how far one can go.
— T.S. Eliot

You don't have to see the whole staircase, just take the first step.
— Martin Luther King, Jr.

Arise and go into the city, and it shall be told thee what thou must do.
— King James Bible, Acts 9:6.

If you try something new, you may succeed or you may fail, you may like it or you may hate it, you may make new friends or even enemies, and you may produce consequences that you never expected — including some you may never even know about. Trying something new is a risk. You don't know in advance what the result will be.

However, if you want to be *absolutely sure* about your results, there is one thing you can do — nothing! When you do nothing, you can be sure that nothing will result.

So there are some big advantages to taking risks. "Yes," we can hear you thinking, "but what if I fail, or what if I hate it?" That could happen, but what if it did? One of the biggest blocks to action is the fear of failure, but is failure all that bad? Sure, failure can mean that you've wasted money, time and effort. But if you are continually learning about yourself and the world around you, there is much to be gained from taking risks and sometimes failing.

It is inevitable that, just as you will sometimes succeed, you also will fail. The story is told that phenomenal athlete Michael Jordan was cut from his high school basketball team. Some people believe that the ability to take failure in stride is the key to success. We like Winston Churchill's attitude: "Success is the ability to go from one failure to another with no loss of enthusiasm."

Bill Walsh, the great football coach, put it this way: "Many people erroneously think they have only one chance to succeed in their life's work, and if they miss that chance, they are doomed to failure. If they learn from past mistakes, they will be better able to take full advantage of the next opportunity when it presents itself."

Trying something that does not work out as hoped may be unpleasant, but it can provide a valuable learning experience. You can gain in one way, even while you are disappointed in another way.

We're not advocating that you take foolish risks. Of course you don't want to go sky diving without a parachute! In this chapter we will see how a number of different people took risks — sometimes the outcomes were favorable, sometimes unfavorable, and sometimes unknown.

Take Risks That Are Likely to Pay Off

Everyone loves a success story, so we're going to begin with some stories from people who took risks that paid off.

You should already know how to perform on a job before you apply for it or accept it, right? That's the popular wisdom, but we know one highly successful businesswoman who said, "I've never accepted a job I already knew how to do." If you already know how to do the job going in, you're not going to enjoy the satisfaction of accomplishing something brand new. People often have fond memories of their first successes in school, business, athletics and romance.

DILBERT By Scott Adams

Reprinted with Permission of United Feature Syndicate, Inc.

Take risks — but not foolish risks.

Instead of thinking that you must have already mastered a new job before you even begin, it is better to think of the new job as a learning opportunity. Malik's experience is a case in point.

"Who's Going to Train Us?"

I was working for a non-profit agency that helped immigrants and refugees. We were going broke. I volunteered to help write grant requests to foundations, corporations and public agencies. One request that paid off resulted in IBM donating a complex computer system to our agency. Everyone then asked, "Who is going to learn how to use the computer and then train the rest of us to use it?" I knew nothing about computers, but I volunteered.

IBM offered free self-study training classes as part of their donation of hardware. I was curious about computers and thought this would be an excellent opportunity for me to learn about computers for free. I felt confident that if I could learn to use the computer myself, then I could readily teach others.

As soon as I completed my self-paced training, I started to develop a training class for Asian immigrants and refugees who were often applying for data entry clerical jobs. Learning from my own trials and errors with several pilot classes, I was able to develop a beginning and advanced data entry skills class. I later applied these same skills in developing and teaching computer skills in a business setting. I've been involved in computer-related training ever since that time.

Note the actions that Malik took:
- He volunteered to help write requests for grants.
- He volunteered to learn, even though he knew nothing about computers.
- He signed up for self-study classes.
- He was optimistic that he could teach others once he learned himself.
- He developed a class for immigrants and refugees.
- He taught data entry skills.
- He transferred his new skills to a job he obtained in business.

Malik was not afraid to try new activities just because he did not already know how to do them. He tried them, he liked them, and he benefited from them.

Be Prepared for Unexpected Opportunities

You never know in advance just which event might lead to an interesting opportunity. Jasmine allowed herself to accompany a friend to a conference which radically changed her career direction.

"For Some Reason, I Took Along My Resume..."

I had just moved back to Los Angeles after an eleven-year absence and was stalled in the career search. I had many skills, but I was uncertain how to focus my search or which skills would serve me best. I had done Shiatsu massage for several years and had run a small house painting business before that. Toward the end of my thirties, I returned to school. While in school I taught English as a foreign language to help make ends meet, but teaching was not one of my "target" careers.

A friend who had also recently relocated was interested in teaching, and she asked that I accompany her to a conference aimed at recruiting people of color for independent schools. As a woman of color myself, I was interested in attending, primarily to see who would be there. But for some reason, I decided to take along a few copies of each of three versions of my resume (one for massage, one for a research position, and one for general use).

At the conference, I ran into a recent acquaintance who seemed delighted to see me. She had just spoken with the people from a college prep/technical arts high school, and she immediately thought of me. My very diverse work history seemed a "perfect profile" for a position there. Over my protests, she walked me directly over to the booth to meet the assistant headmaster, whom I immediately liked. He asked for a resume to keep on file.

Three months later he contacted me when a temporary position opened up as a librarian while the permanent librarian was on sabbatical. I ended up working there for six years and grew enormously, both professionally and personally.

Jasmine's story illustrates some important points:
- She developed a friendly outgoing manner that made friends and acquaintances delighted to see her.
- She accepted when a friend invited her to go to a conference.
- She took a risk, knowing that she might be wasting both her time and her money.
- She took another risk by going along to meet the assistant headmaster.
- She went prepared, with three different versions of her resume.
- She selected the right one to leave with the assistant headmaster.
- She took a chance on a temporary job.
- She built it into a full-time position.
- She remained and prospered for six years.

Jasmine created her own luck, took risks, and made them pay off.

You may learn a hobby or skill that you could build into a business of your own. Sheila discovered quite by accident that she had a money-making skill — or maybe Sheila's actions played the crucial role. Was this *happenstance?*

"Why Don't You Make More and Sell Them?"

Soon after getting married while I was at the university, my husband was a new accountant. We were very poor. I couldn't get a part time job.

My husband needed new ties to wear to work, but we couldn't afford to buy them. Since I had learned how to sew, I got out my sewing machine and made him a tie.

One of his colleagues at work really liked the tie and said, "Why don't you make more of these and sell them here?"

I made a bunch of ties and arranged to take them to my husband's workplace at lunchtime. I sold nearly all of them and came home with lots of money.

That was the beginning of a small business I ran for two-and-a-half years before going overseas. That experience of running a business and being self-reliant has had a major impact on every area of my career and life in general.

Sheila capitalized on a skill she had initially learned as a child and took the initiative in volunteering to sew a necktie for her husband. She listened to the positive feedback she received about her work. She could have discounted it with self-deprecating comments such as, "They are just being polite." She took a big risk in making a number of neckties and taking them to his workplace. His coworkers might not have bought them. She responded to the initial success by expanding her business. Small successes build on themselves. The self-confidence she gained from that experience has stayed with her ever since.

Discover Something Unknown to You Before

One of the many disadvantages of making an early career decision is that you are likely to overlook occupations that are unknown to you. Fortunately for Rachel, no such predestined goal blocked her view of new possibilities.

"I Had No Idea"

When I graduated from college, I had no idea what I wanted to do. It took me a year to find my first job because there was a bad economic recession at the time. During that year of searching I stumbled upon an occupation that I did not know even existed — foreign rights in book publishing. Although I was reluctant to accept an invitation to a company's cocktail party, I went and met a woman there who told me about this work, and it sounded fascinating to me. It involves negotiating contracts with foreign publishers who want to translate American books into their languages and sell them in other countries. It involves communicating with a variety of interesting people from all over the world. One publishing company offered me an entry level position, but then had to cut costs. I was disappointed — to say the least. I took a secretarial job at another publishing company just to make ends meet. They sold books in the U.S. only. One day I happened to get on the elevator with the president of the company. I said to him, "I'll bet our company could increase its profits tremendously if we could sell our books in other countries."

"Yes, but in many countries the people don't speak English."

"We could contract with foreign publishers to translate our books."

"We've never done that before."

"Would you let me try to see what I could arrange?"

"Sure. But check with me when you find out what's possible."

I obtained a directory of foreign publishers, picked out three likely prospects, wrote them a letter along with a catalog of the books we published. All three expressed interest in translating one or more of our books. That's how I got started as the foreign rights coordinator.

Note the ways in which Rachel seized on a chance meeting and then took the initiative:
- She accepted a party invitation even though she knew few of the attendees.
- She engaged a stranger in conversation.
- She applied for jobs she did not get.
- She accepted a secretarial job even though that was not what she wanted.

- She happened to meet the president of the publishing company in the elevator.
- She seized the opportunity to propose her idea.
- She volunteered to implement the idea herself!

Take Risks That May Fail

Advocates of risk taking need to remember that the stories do not always have happy endings. The following story comes from Martin in New Zealand.

Running for Public Office

I had planned a career in politics, and for many years was involved in politics at a local level. When the local member of Parliament retired, I took the chance offered and sought the nomination which would lead to my becoming the candidate at the next election. It was a reasonably safe constituency and I was almost certain to be elected.

The great day of candidate selection arrived and I competed with six others for the nomination. It was a race between me and one of those other six, but most people thought I would get it. The local radio station rang me the day before to arrange an interview with me after I had won the election.

Much to my shock and amazement, I was not selected. My political ambitions collapsed in one afternoon. I knew I would never try this again — my political career was over.

Martin's high hopes were dashed by the outcome of the election. He took a risk he considered reasonable, but the voters thought otherwise. Now he declares that his political ambitions have ended forever.

Should Martin renounce politics forever because of one election? We're not in a position to advise him, but it would be fair to point out that history is filled with prominent political leaders — Abraham Lincoln and Winston Churchill among them — who lost many an election before winning a big one.

It is easy to let a defeat sap your energy and enthusiasm, especially if you take it personally. However, there is a more objective way of looking at this: What did Martin actually lose? Before the election he was not a candidate for Parliament; after the election he was not a candidate for Parliament. Objectively speaking, he was no worse off after the election than he was before, except, perhaps for some bruised feelings. We know that bruised feelings are hard to bear, but he had made a noble try and can take pride in his constructive efforts to participate in public affairs. The fact that taking one risk did not work out as desired should not dissuade anyone from refusing to take any more risks. Maybe Martin will change his mind and try again. Maybe someday he will become Prime Minister of New Zealand. Maybe he will turn his attention to other arenas. Risking and failing is not necessarily a catastrophe. Thomas Moore, in his book *Care of the Soul*, stated that, "We can learn more from our failures than our successes." Perhaps, as the hurt feelings subside, Martin will analyze what happened and learn some valuable insights that will guide him in the future.

Take Risks with Unknown Outcomes

Many of our actions in life have an impact on others that we never know. Words spoken by teachers and parents can have a powerful impact on children — sometimes years later. But the teachers and parents who uttered those words may never know.

Even strangers may meet, converse, and part having had a significant but unknown impact on the other. You can learn, and help others learn, in brief unexpected encounters.

You are not only the recipient of unplanned events — you also are the instigator of unplanned events which may have an impact on others. We all have the power to provide encouragement and support to the people with whom we come in contact. Chantal describes an experience she had while walking through a run-down section of Los Angeles.

"I'm Off the Track — Help Me Get Back On"

I am walking down the street, heading home, at a pretty fast clip. I spot a school on a side street so I walk up and take a look at it. Now I'm back on the main drag and I pass a young man fiddling around a car parked on the street.

"Hey," he says, "don't you teach at Wabash?"

"No, I don't teach there," I say, "but you're right, I have taught."

"Oh yeah." He is walking beside me. He has to take long strides because I accelerate my pace. I tell him a little about my teaching experience and then ask him about his education.

"I've been in the Job Corps, and I was sent to Utah for some training."

"Well, that sounds good."

"Not really. I knew everything they taught me."

"But you got a free trip to Utah. That was good."

"Yeah, but it was really a waste of time for me. My uncle had taught me all the building trades. I knew almost everything they taught. My uncle knew how to do everything. He laid out the drainage system for the whole Los Angeles area. He understood how it should be done, and he was part of getting the whole job completed."

"Wow," I said, "What are you doing now?

"I'm on G. R."

"It seems to me that you can do better than being on general relief. You are an intelligent man."

Now we are at a busy intersection, and it would be a good time to part. We both wait for the light to change, and then we cross the street together.

"I'm trying to get SSI," he says.

"No, you don't want SSI; that's a dead end street. You need a good job."

"I can't get work. I had a job as an apartment maintenance man, but the guy who managed the apartment lost his job and so I lost mine."

"That's no big deal. You have those skills. People can really use them."

"Yeah, but nobody wants to hire me."

"It doesn't sound hopeless to me. It may take a little effort but you could do it."

"Yeah," he says, not really convinced. I am still walking at my brisk pace, and he is wearing out. He sits down on a beat-up bench at the side of a little store as we continue talking.

"And I've got a record with the police," he tells me.

"What for?"

"I was partying with some friends and it got a little out of control. When the police arrived I didn't behave as respectfully as I should have. There was a misunderstanding. They asked me something and I stood up. Then they accused me of assaulting an officer — which I did not do!!"

"That happens," I say. "Everybody knows how that can happen. You can explain it away." We were walking again and discussing run-ins with the police.

"Are you sure you have to get yourself in those situations? How old are you?"

"I'm thirty-two, and I'm trying to stay out of trouble like my older brother; he's married and has a son."

"Good. Life is hard enough without having to deal with the police."

Then he stops and points to a slanted part line in his hair. "That's from a bullet, but I believe in God so I wasn't killed."

I look at the scar. "Wow! That was a close call. God wants you alive. He's got something he wants you to do."

"Yeah, and look." He lifts up his shirt and shows me a torso full of scars. "These are stab wounds."

He points to some. I look them over and point to others he can't see on his back.

"That's a lot," I say. "You don't have to live like that. You're a grown man. You've got to set a good example for your nephew. You're too intelligent to be living like that."

"Yeah." Still not convinced. "It's just that I need, well, it's just hard, if someone would just. . . ."

"You can do it," I said. "You're a smart man, a capable man and a skilled man."

"You keep telling me I'm intelligent."

"You are intelligent. You came from a family of intelligence. How about your uncle? Wasn't he intelligent?"

"Yeah, but if I just had . . . Look, tell me your phone number so I can get in touch with you."

"Young man," I said in my best teacher voice, "You can't get in touch with me. I do not have a telephone." Then I thought for a moment about whether I should say more and blurted out, "And I don't have a car and I don't have a television set."

There was a hushed silence. I felt I had said more than I realized.

"You are living the way God wants us to live," he says quietly.

"And you can too. You've got a lot on the ball. You can do a lot more than you're doing now."

He gave me an uncertain nod of agreement, and I decided that it was time to make my exit.

"How can I see you again?" he asks.

"Oh, I'll be back this way, and the next time I see you I want to hear good news, not bad. I want to hear how you're winning, not losing."

I am walking away from him and talking at him.

"You're intelligent; you can do it. Now you win!" As I walk away from him I find myself shouting to him, "Win!! Yes, you can!! Good luck!!"

It took me about a week to absorb that whole experience. Then I realized that his key line was, "My uncle laid out the drainage system with others for the whole of L.A." He might as well have said, "I come from a family of intelligence, competence and responsibility, but I'm off the track. Help me get back on."

My self-disclosure about not owning a telephone, car or TV seemed to have elevated his esteem for me and deepened the truth of my other statements. Trying to live simply in a chaotic world of distractions, temptations and frustrations apparently gave me a little credibility.

And, no, I've never seen him again.

Everyone needs to hear some encouraging words, and we all should be offering them to others. Chantal took a risk in striking up a conversation with a strange man on the street. Chantal saw potential in the young man and tried to encourage it. Did he really want her encouraging words? Or was he simply looking for a handout? We will never know his true motivation nor the effect that Chantal's encouragement might have had on him. At a minimum he might have learned that he was capable of eliciting encouragement from a stranger.

The story illustrates that encouragement can have an impact on both its giver and receiver. Note Chantal's key actions:

- She took a risk by engaging in conversation with a stranger on the street.
- She repeatedly told him he was intelligent.
- She encouraged him to get a job and get off welfare ("general relief").
- She praised his previous attempt to get training.
- She elicited stories of his life.

- She said the police record could be explained.
- She capitalized on his belief in God by asserting that God must need him to do something.
- She said he had skills that others would need.
- She asserted that the situation was not hopeless.
- She shared some details of her own life style without revealing the contact information he had requested.

The conversation obviously did have an impact on Chantal. It had some impact on the young man too, since he obviously wanted to see her again. She had provided comfort to someone in distress and learned more about the difficulties some young men face in that part of town. She shared her own philosophy about living a simple life and felt validated by his response to it. The experience had an emotional impact such that Chantal wanted to write a detailed account of it and share it with others. Chantal's life was certainly changed in small but important ways by the risk she took. Whether the man's life was changed we will never know, but Chantal's support and encouragement could still be playing an important role in his life.

Use Media to Suggest Unlikely Career Opportunities

Some of the best ways of locating career opportunities may not be obvious at first. Even TV programs can suggest possibilities if you keep your eyes open as Marita did.

Surfin' the Silk

I saw a web site on a talk show that dealt with custom clothes, so I surfed to the site and saw that the woman used to live in my hometown.

I emailed her to see if there was a store where I could see her clothing and hand-painted fabrics.

I told her I'm a silk painter.

She was looking for a silk painter.

She sent fabric and sketches.

I duplicated the designs and sent them back.

It may be the beginning of my own hand-painted clothing business.

We don't know what reaction the woman will give Marita. We don't know whether Marita will start her own hand-painted clothing business or not. We do know that Marita took a number of creative initiatives starting with her alert observation of a web site URL on the credits of a TV show. One never knows from whence may come the next clue in the mystery of life.

Stay in Touch with Friends and Colleagues

Building and maintaining good relationships with other people is an important component for job success. You can maintain relationships with people you like and respect by keeping in touch with them by phone, mail, or email. Your reputation with them depends on how well you follow-up on your promises and honor your commitments. Hope's experience illustrates how you can antagonize one supervisor but build good relationships with another.

Building and Maintaining Bridges

I was working as a receptionist at a high-tech company. The people were nice to me, but I hated the work. I applied for a transfer into the human resources department, but the manager there told me I was not right for the job because I "...didn't have a sense of urgency." So I called up a temp agency and asked them if they had any positions in human resource departments at other companies.

I interviewed for two positions and received an offer for one of them. I was very excited to find a new job. Unfortunately, to get the new position, I had to start right away. That meant that I had to take the risk of quitting my old job without giving the normal two-weeks notice. My boss was angry at me for quitting so abruptly and told me he would never take me back, but I was excited about my new opportunity.

The next morning I went to my new job, bright and early, only to find out they had decided to give the position to someone internally! So I had no job and no way of going back! I had burned my bridges.

I was scared and angry at what had just happened. The temp agency felt bad about it and offered some short-term positions while I searched for a long-term one. I needed to earn some money, so I agreed to take one- or two-day assignments doing filing. I was assigned to a computer products company doing some filing and organizing for their human resources department.

After I'd worked there for a few days, they decided to keep me on indefinitely! My supervisor there was very supportive and encouraging. Later on she left the company and we kept in touch. A year later she called me with a job opportunity with more potential and higher pay, and this is where I am today.

Hope had more options than she might have realized. She was told she had to start the new job right away, but she could have tried to negotiate additional time on the grounds that she wanted to honor her commitment to her present employer. Such loyalty could have been perceived as desirable by the new employer. She might also have requested the new job offer in writing. She might also have told her present employer about the job offer and negotiated improved pay and conditions where she was.

However, Hope did take some positive actions. When she finally landed a temporary job, she must have done some good work because they wanted to keep her. She developed a good relationship with her new supervisor and maintained it for a year even after the supervisor had left the company. When the supervisor needed additional help, she remembered Hope and knew how to contact her because Hope had maintained the relationship.

Solicit Encouragement from Others

Encouragement from others may help you take risks you otherwise would avoid. Your job is to elicit that encouragement. Oscar's story illustrates the power of showing people your work, while the following story — Claudio's — illustrates the importance of sharing your hopes and fears with others.

Self-Discovery — Stupendous Success

I was lucky to have a boss who saw my potential and redesigned my work duties to take advantage of my natural, but undiscovered potential.

I had received a B.S. degree in biochemistry and got a job as a lab tech doing genetic research. In college, I never took a course in computers and had no real interest in them. As part of my new job however, I was assigned to graph results in a computer spreadsheet. At first I was not interested in the task, but I got more intrigued with the process as I got into it. I began exploiting the graphing capabilities of the software and showing the results to my boss.

He took notice of my developing interest, purchased some database software, and asked if I would be interested in learning how to create a database system for our DNA bank. Two classes and four months later, I had completed a robust system, published a paper on it (also by happenstance, the magazine I submitted it to was looking for articles for an upcoming Biocomputing issue, unbeknownst to me), and subsequently received over fifty requests for my software. What a self-discovery and what a stupendous success for a first try!

Oscar thought he was not interested in computers until he actually was required to use one for his graphing assignment. His boss took notice of his capabilities and encouraged him by giving him a yet more complicated assignment using computers. Oscar was fortunate to have a boss who recognized his potential, but Oscar took many actions that communicated that potential to his boss. Oscar responded to the risky challenge, and his career became more satisfying for him.

Claudio got help from a chance encounter with an encouraging stranger.

"No Money, No SATs, No Direction"

I was a new immigrant to America living in New England and not working because I had no green card. One day by chance I met a woman and we started talking about life in America. She explained to me how she had moved here from Germany and how she decided to find out about going to college.

I was twenty-three-years old, and I had never attended college. I thought of every barrier possible. I had no money, no SAT scores, no career direction, no proficiency in English. She said that I could apply to the nearest community college without having all these qualifications. At first I was skeptical because I didn't want to take the risk of being rejected. Then I started thinking about the possibility. I went to the Community College to find out if it was possible. I wrote back to my high school in Europe to get my results and applied. Sure enough, she was right — I was accepted. I completed the two-year college, went on to a four-year college with a scholarship and now am enrolled in graduate school.

I am sure that if I had not met her and she had not been so insistent that age, qualifications, and money were not insurmountable barriers, I would not have persisted. I know her encouragement changed the course of my life.

Claudio received encouragement from a woman who had been through the process herself. Although he attributes the meeting to "chance," his own interpersonal skills played an important role in getting this encouragement. While he generously credits the woman for changing his life, he did engage her in conversation, shared experiences in common, discussed college possibilities, and overcame his skepticism to find out about and risk applying to college. Credit for his subsequent success can be attributed, not only to his supportive mentor, but also to his own ability and hard work.

You can give and receive encouragement in several ways: (1) You can do your work in a way that will be noticed by other people who are in a position to help you; (2) You can talk with other people about your fears, hopes and dreams; (3) You can demonstrate your interest and concern with the lives of others by listening to their hopes and fears and providing active help when asked — or even sometimes when not asked.

Assume Your Interests Will Change

Trying to make a firm decision on a permanent occupation may give you a feeling of security, but actually it is fraught with peril. One danger is that the occupation you choose in advance may not be nearly as satisfying as you expected. Another danger is that the occupation itself may disappear in our fast-changing career marketplace. And it's possible — even likely — that your interests may change. You may discover something far more fascinating as the result of a whole series of unrelated and unplanned events. This is what happened to Jill.

"Signs of Life in Outer Space"

Jill Tarter, an only child, grew up hunting and fishing with her father. She felt she was her "father's son." Her father died when she was twelve, but she had made up her mind to be an engineer. She received a bachelor's degree in engineering but found the work unsatisfying. She went back to school in theoretical physics and happened to take a course in star formation. She said, "That was just it as far as I was concerned, a kind of 'Eureka!' experience." She obtained a job programming a computer to control a spectrometer package. She worked for some years until the computer became obsolete.

The old computer was then given to an X-ray astronomer named Stu Bowyer who had no money but wanted to analyze some astronomical data for signs of artificial signals. He didn't know how to operate the computer but was told that Jill had once used it. They met and began working together. He gave her a book on the search for extraterrestrial intelligence, and she was fascinated with the idea. When funding became available, she was recruited for SETI (the Search for Extraterrestrial Intelligence). According to John Billingham, she was chosen because she possessed three qualities: "...(1) her competence, experience and training...; (2) her extraordinary perseverance; and (3) her ability to communicate; she is both articulate and eloquent."

When Jill started her career she had no idea that she would someday be searching the heavens for signs of extraterrestrial intelligence. She had decided to be an engineer. Engineering did not work out for her as she had hoped. Nevertheless, she had learned some valuable skills in the process.

Trying something that does not work is never a total loss. You not only discover something you do NOT want to do, you pick up some valuable skills that may be useful somewhere else. Keep trying different alternatives until something clicks.

Leigh Weimers, "Homing in on any E.T.s out there." San Jose Mercury News, January 3, 1999. pp. 1G, 4G. Reprinted by permission.

Since you can never be sure in advance which activities will satisfy you, you need to develop an experimental attitude:

- Take risks that are likely to pay off.
- Be prepared for unexpected opportunities.
- Discover something unknown to you before.

- Take risks that may fail.
- Take risks with unknown outcomes.
- Use media to suggest unlikely career opportunities.
- Stay in touch with friends and colleagues.
- Solicit encouragement from others.
- Assume your interests will change.

Find Some New Things to Try

A common myth is that you need to have clear goals before you launch a new venture or try a new activity. In fact, goals can be formed and changed while you are engaging in a new activity. You can't really know whether you like it until you try it. A new activity may not necessarily give you just what you want — it could give you even more than you expected. If you are dissatisfied with the way your life is going, here are some questions designed to stimulate your thinking about alternatives you might want to try.

1. Are there some activities you would enjoy regardless of how skillful you might be?

   ___ Walking?   ___ Gourmet cooking?
   ___ Cross-country skiing?   ___ Genealogy?
   ___ Working crossword puzzles?   ___ Sailing?
   ___ Woodworking?   ___ Video production?
   ___ Wilderness backpacking?   ___ Golfing?
   ___ Volunteer community service?   ___ (You name it):

   _____

2. What do you need for an activity to be satisfying?

   ___ Improving your own skill   ___ Beating someone else
   ___ The activity itself   ___ (You name it):

   _____

3. Give your imagination free rein for a moment. Think of an activity you would really love. What might it be?

   ___ Playing a musical instrument?
   ___ Running for political office?
   ___ Studying space travel?

___ Building your own house?
___ Speaking a foreign language?
___ (You name it): _____

4. The people who are successful at any of these activities were not born skillful at them. They learned to be successful — one step at a time. If you really wanted to engage in a particular activity, what would be the first step you would need to take? _____
    _____

5. Would you be willing to try taking that first step?
    ___ Yes, I have nothing to lose and might enjoy it.
    ___ No, I might not succeed. (Better read chapter 5!)

6. When will you take that first step?
    ___ Today at _____ AM/PM
    ___ Tomorrow at _____ AM/PM
    ___ (Name a specific date): _____

7. Telling someone else about your intent to take an action increases the likelihood that you will actually do it. With whom will you share your intent to take that first step? _____
    _____

Making the Most of Happenstance

We encourage you to try new activities even when you don't know the outcomes. You will find some fascinating adventures, and you will also have some failures. Both success and failure are part of the fun of living. We don't want you to worry about the failures, as we shall convince you in the next chapter.

Chapter 5

Go Ahead and Make Mistakes

Fall seven times, stand up eight.
— Japanese proverb

No matter how far you've gone down the wrong road, turn back.
— Turkish proverb

Never be afraid to try. No one ever died of embarrassment.
— Nina Jacobson

Fear of making mistakes keeps some people from doing what they really want to do. The origin of the fear is understandable. So much of schooling involves getting the "right" answer. The wrong answer leads to low grades, a loss of self-esteem, and the worry that a successful future may be in jeopardy. The system requires that, in most classrooms, mistakes are to be punished by teachers.

Why then are we encouraging you to make mistakes? Because there is something much worse than making a mistake — doing nothing out of fear that you *might* make a mistake.

For some people, the fear of making mistakes relates to a quest for perfection. These individuals would like to get 100 percent on every test in school, get straight As in all their courses, win every athletic event they enter, get the perfect job, become an instant success, and find the perfect mate for a lifetime of bliss. And who can really blame anyone for feeling this way? We live in a society where "winning is the only thing," whether it's the stock market, the Academy Awards, or the Super Bowl. Unfortunately doing your best — and even coming in second — isn't seen as much of an accomplishment.

FRANK & ERNEST By Bob Thaves

Trying to be perfect is a recipe for unhappiness.

There's a lot to be said for doing your best, but striving for perfection is a recipe for unhappiness. You are guaranteed to fail, since no human being is perfect, not even you. The best musical artists have an off night every concert tour. Professional baseball players seldom hit successfully more than one time in three. Top tennis players make numerous unforced errors. Winning political candidates don't get elected unanimously — except in dictatorships! There is no reason to expect that you will be perfect in everything you do. Naturally you want to do your best, to strive for excellence, but perfection remains an impossible standard.

We want you to develop a new attitude about making mistakes. *Making mistakes is inevitable.* Learning anything new requires you to make mistakes, and it's perfectly OK to make mistakes. This chapter concentrates on helping you recognize two main points:

- Making mistakes is common, normal, and instructive.
- Learning from your mistakes will help you to become successful.

Don't Be Afraid to Fail

The following list has been used by college basketball coach Don Meyer to inspire his players:

You've failed many times, although you don't remember.
You fell down the first time you tried to walk.
You almost drowned the first time you tried to swim.

Did you hit the ball the first time you swung the bat?

Heavy hitters, the ones who hit the most home runs, also strike out a lot.

R. H. Macy failed seven times before his store in New York caught on.

Novelist John Creasey got 753 rejection slips before he published 564 books.

Babe Ruth hit 714 home runs, but he also struck out 1,330 times.

The message is, don't worry about failure.

Worry instead about the chances you miss when you don't even try.

Make Use of Your Mistakes

Mistakes are not only normal, they are valuable. They can teach you important lessons, and sometimes they lead to outcomes that are even better than the outcomes you hoped for.

The willingness to take action and try something new may well result in some mistakes, but sometimes those mistakes lead to unanticipated outcomes. Consider the case of Cameron.

The Wrong Address

I arrived in London after a period working in Europe and was in need of money so began looking for work. I had no idea what type of work I would prefer. I went to a notice board and noted a small handwritten notice outlining a position available in a sport store for a sales assistant.

I telephoned the number. The woman asked me a few questions regarding my background in skiing, climbing and camping and told me a little about the business. Then she said to pop into the shop for an interview and gave me an address on this small street in central London.

I found the street without too many problems and noted a sport store with a sign on the door: "Staff wanted apply within." I went in, introduced myself, and said I had been speaking to a woman (I had forgotten her name) about the vacancy and had been invited for an interview.

"Oh, that would be Julie, the assistant manager. She is at lunch but come in and meet the manager."

GARFIELD By Jim Davis

Learn from your mistakes.

The interview that followed was odd to say the least. It went something like this:

Manager: "Well, what do you know about our business?"

Cameron: "I understand you have branches in Leeds and Bristol."

Manager: "No, we have branches in Manchester and Cardiff."

Cameron: "I understand you specialize in climbing equipment."

Manager: "Well, no, we don't sell a lot of climbing equipment but specialize more in general camping equipment."

And so it went on. I was feeling a bit foolish actually. However I got the job and left the store happily.

On leaving the store I looked across the road to find another sport store. I then checked my notebook to find I had gone to the wrong store.

Two sport stores on a street of fourteen businesses both wanting staff! However, as it turned out, I had stumbled into a better job, better pay and better working conditions.

I worked in the store for nine or ten months altogether and became friendly with the manager. Only on my last day did I reveal my error to the manager. He also had thought it a strange interview!

Cameron started out doing everything right:
- He found an advertisement for a job to his liking.
- He took the initiative to phone.
- He asked some questions about the business as well as sharing his own experience.
- His only mistake was to show up at the wrong door.
- The manager hired him (probably impressed by his initiative and manner), despite Cameron's obvious ignorance of the business.

Cameron's mistake resulted in a better job than he would have had if he had entered the right door. We are not advocating that you deliberately make mistakes in showing up at unintentional locations! We are saying that making occasional mistakes is not necessarily fatal, and that you may be able to adapt to the unexpected situation in positive ways. Cameron did not confess his error until it was time for him to quit the job. Both he and the manager thought the interview was strange, but Cameron had sold the manager on his ability to do the job anyway.

Make Use of Other People's Mistakes

You are not the only one who will be making mistakes, of course. You can treat other people's mistakes as opportunities, not as annoyances. That's what Candice did.

"Wrong Number, Please"

I had been a registered nurse (R.N.). When I experienced severe burnout and couldn't take it any more, I resigned from a position I had held for over eighteen years. I had no new job lined up.

I volunteered to teach an upcoming class being offered by my former employer because of a desire to stay connected with my former colleagues, occupy myself, and have one more item to put on my resume. I came upon this opportunity while attending a party. When a colleague mentioned how much she enjoyed teaching one day a week at a local college in the nursing program, I took that idea to heart. When I saw an ad in the Sunday paper for a full-time nursing instructor at a local community college, I applied.

The screening process for that job had not yet commenced, but one morning I got a call from the college asking if I would like to fill in as a substitute teacher. For some reason I said yes, taught for four weeks, and loved it.

When the instructor of record returned, my job was over. A few days later, however, she accidentally phoned me (a wrong number — she thought she was calling someone else), but I recognized her voice and said, "Hi, Vi!" We got to talking, and she asked if I was working yet or had been hired at the college to which I had applied. When I said no, she told me she knew of several job openings, and she gave me three referrals! Just two days later, the head of my volunteer project called to offer me a part-time paid position.

When Candice picked up the phone, she could have replied, "Sorry, you have the wrong number." Instead, recognizing the caller's voice, she engaged her in an extended conversation and obtained the names and phone numbers of people with job openings of the type she had just recently learned to love. Note the proactive steps Candice took:

- She volunteered for a teaching project with her former employer.
- She attended a party with former colleagues.
- She engaged at least one of them in conversation and found out about community college teaching.
- She searched the newspaper for relevant ads and found one.
- She applied for the position.
- She agreed to work as a substitute teacher (not her first choice).
- She evidently did good work as a volunteer and as a substitute teacher.
- She struck up a conversation with someone who phoned her by mistake and learned about additional job openings.

Gain Inspiration from Another Person's Mistake

Sometimes admitting to a mistake can be the best thing that you can do. It can even be an unlikely source of inspiration to other people. Kent's story illustrates this point.

Even Teachers Make Mistakes

I always thought that teachers were perfect and knew everything. Throughout my twelve years in school I saw that my fellow students and I seldom got 100 percent on the teachers' tests, but obviously the teachers knew the answers to all the questions. (It has taken me years to realize that the reason they knew the answers was because they had written the questions and had made out the scoring key themselves!) While I thought it would be fun be a teacher, I never thought I was qualified because I knew I was not perfect.

In the twelfth grade I took a course in American Government from the only teacher in my small school who had a master's degree. One day in class he was explaining the electoral college system of electing U.S. presidents: "A state allocates the number of electoral votes to each candidate in proportion to the popular votes each candidate receives."

I raised my hand and stated very politely, "I don't think that is correct, Mr. H. I think the candidate who receives the largest number of popular votes in a state gets all the electoral votes from that state."

"No, Kent, the electoral votes are apportioned to the different candidates."

"That does seem like a reasonable way to do it, sir, but actually the system is set up so that all the electoral votes go to the highest vote-getter."

"Well, I think you are wrong, Kent, but I'll double-check on it and get back to you tomorrow."

The next day he announced in class, "Yesterday, Kent corrected me on the way electoral votes are allocated. He was absolutely right. I had made a mistake. Thank you, Kent, for noticing the error and calling it to our attention."

I was stunned. I had never known a teacher to make a mistake and acknowledge it before. I thought to myself, "If a teacher with a master's degree can make a mistake and still be a successful teacher, then maybe I, with all my imperfections, could be a successful teacher too." My teacher's mistake and his gracious acknowledgement of it were inspiring for me. I went into the field of teaching and have enjoyed my work in education tremendously. Thank you, Mr. Hawbaker, for letting me know that you were human too.

Recognize That Chance Plays a Part in Every Decision

One of the great myths about career choices is that somewhere there is a perfect job just for you. People searching for the perfect job put themselves under severe stress. They are saying something like this: "What if I make a mistake and choose the wrong occupation??!! Then I'll be perpetually miserable. I must not make this mistake."

They may go to a career counselor and ask, "What occupation would be right for me?" A career counselor answering frankly would have to reply, "There's no such thing as the 'right' occupation for you or anybody else. If there were, I wouldn't know how you could find it. But here's what we can do. We can work together to get you taking actions that will enable you to create a more satisfying life for yourself."

Sometimes the choice between two alternatives is so close that it is exceedingly agonizing to make the choice on any rational grounds. Both alternatives appear to be equally attractive, though not necessarily for the same reasons, so it would seem impossible to make a mistake in choosing either one. Yet if a person believes that there is a perfect job, then only one of the alternatives can be correct, and the other one must be a "mistake."

One way to resolve the dilemma is to openly use a chance mechanism, such as the flip of a coin, to make the decision. If the choice is that close, then either alternative is equally attractive and the specific alternative doesn't matter. Here are two cases in which the flip of a coin was used to make a decision — and the different ways in which the decider then proceeded.

English? Or Psychology?

Samuel Messick became one of the world's leading psychologists in the field of educational measurement. When he died, his obituary contained this account of his early life:

Sam Messick grew up in Philadelphia, the youngest child and only son of his father, Samuel, a police officer, and his mother, Caroline, a factory seamstress. His academic achievements resulted in a full scholarship to the University of Pennsylvania — an offer that was rescinded when the award sponsors decided that Sam's family was too poor to make good use of the scholarship. Fortunately, the organization relented in response to vigorous protest from Sam's high school.

Except for a toss of a coin, Sam might never have become a renowned measurement expert. At the University of Pennsylvania, he was torn between majoring in psychology or English. His solution was to flip a coin. . . . psychology won and Sam earned not only his bachelor's degree in the field, but also his master's (1953) and doctorate (1954) from Princeton University.

Advertising? Or Investment Banking?

When he finished his MBA, Ned had two excellent job offers — one in advertising, the other in investment banking. He agonized over the decision. Both offers were attractive, though for different reasons. The time was growing short when he had to make his decision. Both firms were pressing him to decide.

He and his wife were rehashing the decision for the umpteenth time as they were beginning to drive across the Bay Bridge from San Francisco to Oakland. Finally, his wife, Mary, said, "If the decision is that close, why don't you just flip a coin?"

"Good idea," said Ned as their car halted in a traffic jam. "Heads it's advertising, tails it's banking."

He flipped the coin. It came up heads. "OK," he said, "Advertising, here I come."

They drove across the seven-mile span to Oakland in silence. At the other end of the bridge, Ned said, "That was the wrong decision. I want to work in investment banking."

He accepted the job in investment banking and later became involved in the bank's marketing efforts.

Note the difference in these two cases. Sam accepted the coin's decision. Ned rejected it. It's possible that Sam also would have rejected the coin's decision if it had declared English as his major. We'll never know. However, in both cases flipping a coin helped to overcome the logjam of competing alternatives. Flipping the coin helped Ned to clarify his feelings. He found that sometimes making any decision that enables you to move ahead is better than struggling with the alternatives forever.

NON SEQUITUR By Wiley

Making choices in the real world is not as easy as you might like.

The coin toss does not actually make the decision. You still make the decision. Pretending that you have turned control over to chance puts the agony behind you. The decision has been made. Now you can focus on how you feel about it. Sometimes you really know deep inside what you prefer, but you wish someone else would take responsibility for making the decision. Making the coin responsible, even temporarily, relieves you of that responsibility and frees you up to listen to your own deepest wishes. Then you can choose to overrule the coin — or not.

React to Mistakes Constructively

Perhaps by now we have convinced you that you will be making lots of mistakes and that's OK. The crucial question is how you react to your mistakes. Do you deny your errors, or do you acknowledge them? Do you repeat your mistakes, or do you learn from them? Do you feel devastated and discouraged from your mistakes, or do you resolve to do better next time? The way you react to mistakes makes all the difference in the world. Consider the case of Don Lucas.

Nowhere to Go but Up

Don Lucas grew up in poverty. His father died when Don was eight. His mother had three small children, limited education, was on welfare, and had no job prospects. She packed the three kids into an old sedan and set out from Indiana to California where she obtained a job as a supermarket checker. Don enrolled in a high school in a tough part of town. He describes his town as the spot where drive-by shootings were invented. Few of his classmates ever went to college, and Don did not think about college until his senior year. He had been working from 4:00 to 9:00 p.m. daily at a gas station helping the family to make ends meet.

"One day this great-looking girl walked in. She said she had run out of gas and asked if I could help her. I told her I couldn't leave the station, but I gave her a gas can. She came back later to return the can, driving her brother's hot rod, a classic Ford three-window coupe."

Don and the girl, Sally, became friends. Sally planned to go to college and urged Don to do the same. "Had I not met her, maybe I would not have gone on." But with Sally's encouragement Don enrolled in a community college.

In his first semester he earned eighteen units of straight "F" grades. He had enrolled in a heavy load of courses, was working long hours, had a one-hour commute each way, and forgot to withdraw from his classes.

Despite this mistake, another college, closer to home, admitted him on probation. "I worked hard on my grades, took the college prep classes, went to summer school to keep up, and Sally made sure I attended my classes."

"I had to get a job. The only real job I'd had to that point was working in gas stations. I knew cars pretty well, so I tried to get a job selling used cars." He got the job and sold cars between and after classes. He enjoyed the work so much that after a year he got his own used-car dealer's license. He and Sally began buying old cars, fixing them up inside and out, and selling them for a profit. Thus began Don Lucas Automobiles. Don is now founder and CEO of the Lucas Dealership Group, one of the top fifty multiple-franchise car dealerships in the country. He and Sally have been married for over fifty years.

Leigh Weimers, *San Jose Mercury News*, April 4, 1999, pp. 1G, 12G. Reprinted by permission.

Let's take a closer look at how Don responded to his initial college failure:

- He moved to another college closer to home.
- He worked hard on his grades.
- He took college prep classes.
- He went to summer school.
- He responded positively to Sally's encouragement.
- He obtained a more enjoyable part-time job.
- He took the initiative to start his own business capitalizing on his past experience.

He could have repeated his original pattern of college failure. He could have become discouraged and given up. He could have joined a gang and participated in drive-by shootings. He could have taken to alcohol and drugs. He did none of these destructive things. His case represents a classic case of reacting positively to initial mistakes.

Get on with Your Life

When you try something that does not work out as planned, you have two major alternatives: (1) You can persevere and "try, try again," or (2) You can try something else. It's your choice which way you move. In a sense it's fight or flight. There is no one right choice. In either case, you learn from your mistake. Consider Leslie's situation.

Accounting for Failure

I slowly opened the envelope with anticipation and read the words with dread: "We're sorry to inform you that you have failed your clinical comprehensive examination." After years of study and experience in psychology, I had failed a crucial test.

After reading that statement and mourning over it, I began to talk to other people, and to myself, about my experiences in psychology — sifting through the "likes" and "dislikes" of my experience and reflecting on passions of the past. I thought back to the best time in my life. It was not in clinical psychology. It was when I was involved in the orientation program for freshmen in college. What a wonderful time I had watching and helping students grow in the college environment.

This failure experience propelled me to change my career path from clinical child psychologist to higher education administrator where I am now working with considerable satisfaction.

Leslie could have persisted with psychology. She could have asked to retake the examination. She could have learned how her answers fell short. She chose a different path:

- She mourned at first.
- She reflected about her past passions.
- She talked with others about her likes and dislikes.
- She switched to a field that offered her more of what she really enjoyed.

Here's the advice the people in our stories offer about making mistakes:

- Recognize that failure and mistakes are common, normal, and instructive.
- Make use of your mistakes.
- Make use of other people's mistakes.
- Recognize that chance plays a part in every decision.
- React to mistakes constructively.
- Get on with your life.

What's Your Experience with Mistakes?

Making mistakes is normal. Don't let your fear of making mistakes inhibit you from trying something new. Even if it does not work out the way you wanted (few things ever do!), you still will have learned something valuable. You will know better what to do and what not to do in the future. If you don't try, you'll never know.

1. Have you ever made a mistake? Yes ___ No ___

2. Do you know anyone who has never made a mistake?
   Yes ___ No ___

3. If everyone makes mistakes and is still able to survive, should you allow your fear of making mistakes limit your life?
   Yes ___ No ___

4. What action are you are afraid of taking now because you might make a mistake or fail?

_____

_____

5. Suppose you try your best in the action you described in question 4, what would be the worst case scenario for you?

_____

_____

6. How would you handle that worst case if it actually happened?

_____

_____

7. What is the best-case scenario — the outcome that you would want?

_____

_____

8. What would the consequences be for you if you never tried at all?

_____

_____

9. What are you actually going to do?
   a. Give it my best shot
   b. Do something else (What?) _____

   _____

   c. Do nothing

Making the Most of Happenstance

Don't aspire to be a perfectionist. Everyone makes mistakes.

We're not advocating that you intentionally try to make mistakes, of course, but we don't want you to run from them either. If you recognize that mistakes are a normal part of life and that you can benefit from them, many exciting new experiences await you. All you need to do is to start taking action.

Chapter 6

Take Action to Create Your Own Luck

Too many people confine their exercise to jumping to conclusions, running up bills, stretching the truth, bending over backward, lying down on the job, sidestepping responsibility and pushing their luck.
— Author unknown

I'm a great believer in luck — the more I work, the more of it I have.
— Stephen Leacock

Far and away the best prize that life offers is the chance to work hard at work worth doing.
— Theodore Roosevelt

On Spaceship Earth, there are no pilots, only crew.
— Buckminster Fuller

If there is no wind, row.
— Latin Proverb

Did you ever wish that one day your telephone would ring and someone would be calling to offer you the perfect job? Wishing makes for interesting daydreams. No harm comes from wishing — unless wishing is all you do.

The rest of what you do is the important part. You can create your own luck by taking action to increase the chances that you will find a satisfying — maybe not perfect! — job. Since everyone has the same twenty-four hours available each day; it is up to each of us to decide how we will use them. Will you spend your time mulling over the past, wondering why things didn't work out the way you had planned? Or will you spend your time actively engaged in taking action in order to create your opportunities?

In no way are we advocating that you rely on luck alone. Good luck tends to "happen" to people who are engaged in constructive activities. Good luck seldom happens to those who wait passively for the telephone to ring.

ZIGGY © Ziggy & Friends, Inc.

You have to construct the first rungs on your own ladder of success.

Ofra Nevo from Israel said there is an old Jewish joke which illustrates the importance of taking appropriate action if you want good things to happen:

Moishe prays to God every day that God should help him win the lottery.

After praying for three months he becomes desperate and starts arguing with God: "God, I am a poor man. My family needs the money. I am a good observing Jew. I obey all the commandments. Why won't you let me win the lottery?"

Finally a voice from Heaven booms out: "Moishe, first you have to buy a ticket."

This chapter describes and illustrates the types of action that may not win you the lottery but have made a difference in the careers of others and could also make a difference in yours.

Take One Step at a Time

It is said that a trip of a thousand miles begins with just a single step. True, but on the other hand, that first step may, or may not, be in the direction you want to go. It's a good idea to evaluate the results of the first step before taking the second. The following story about Jacob illustrates the step-by-step process.

A Different Color Shirt Can Change Your Life!

Jacob came home every night after work at his bicycle repair business and sat down in front of the television set until it was time for bed. He usually was so exhausted that he could barely muster the energy to push the buttons on his remote control. Finally one day, his wife had seen enough and convinced Jacob to get rid of the television set. With all of his new-found free time, Jacob started baking breads as a hobby. He had often been fascinated with baking but never spent any serious time exploring it as a hobby.

As Jacob tried making various types of breads, cakes, and cookies, he began offering samples to friends. He listened intently to their raves and criticisms. He continually experimented with his recipes to improve the quality.

The hobby soon turned into a passion. Jacob soon found that he couldn't wait to get home from work and begin baking. After several months of refining his recipes, and with the support of his family and friends, Jacob decided to sell his bicycle-repair business and instead open a small bakery.

After he found a site for the bakery, he began baking and selling his breads. He paid visits to the managers of local restaurants and grocery stories and to each one he presented a free loaf of his freshly baked bread.

Soon after, the requests came quickly from several local restaurants wanting to serve his bread. In addition to restaurants, major grocery stores also began stocking his breads, and soon he was expanding the size of his bakery.

When Jacob was asked to explain his success, he replied, "I just changed the color of my T-shirt from black with tire marks to white with bread flour!"

But was it really that simple? If we look more deeply into the events that led to the creation of this successful business, it is clear that certain actions that Jacob took were critical. He took these actions in a cautious series of steps:

- First, Jacob gave up a long-cherished, yet passive activity: staring at the television set. (It probably helped that he received a less-than-subtle push from his wife. Nevertheless, he was the one who actually gave it up. He could easily have bought another television or radio or chosen another passive activity.)
- He became involved with baking, which required effort.
- He chose a hobby that at first had no direct correlation to a "real career." (He was passionate enough that any "real career" opportunity didn't really matter to him at the time.)
- He was willing to share the results of his hobby with his friends.
- He experimented with different recipes.
- He listened to what his friends liked the most.
- He sold the business he hated and opened a business he loved. (Encouragement from friends and family helped convince him.)
- He presented the fruits of his labor to potential clients and customers.
- He expanded the size of his bakery.

Jacob did not start out by declaring, "I want to own a large bakery." Instead, the success of each step led to the next step. He learned as he went. He modestly attributes his success to the color of his shirt, but we know that it was his own actions that did the job.

Realize the Future Starts Right Now

There is an old Turkish proverb that states, "No matter how far you've gone down the wrong road, turn back." Many people find that they have gone down the wrong career path. They may have spent years in preparation and gained much experience in their field, yet they feel trapped — much like Doug.

"I Have Too Much Invested"

Doug met Marcia at a friend's party. The conversation went like this:

"So what do you do?" asked Marcia.

"I'm in real estate," replied Doug.

"How did you happen to get into real estate?"

"Oh, I majored in economics in college, got my MBA degree, and got hired at this small commercial real estate firm in the city."

"How do you like it?"

"I hate it!"

"What's wrong?"

"I just hate the whole process. It's not what I like doing. Always scrambling to find new clients. Always arguing with other people, and most of the arguments are about how much it costs. I don't know how much longer I can stand it."

"Why don't you quit and do something else?" inquired Marcia.

"Oh, no, I couldn't do that — I have too much invested in my real estate training and experience. I just couldn't throw that away."

Doug's situation is not uncommon. Many people feel that the years they have spent in training and gaining experience would be lost if they were to change direction now. *The truth of the matter is that past years are gone no matter what you do now.*

The question you need to ask is, "How can I build a satisfying life for myself starting now?" Your previous experience has taught you some valuable lessons which you may be able to apply in the future, but thinking of the past as an investment which must be maintained traps you.

Even in the stock market investors are repeatedly cautioned not to become "married to a stock." Holding on to a poorly performing stock just because you've already owned it for five years makes no sense if you can now invest that same money in a stock with a more promising future. And when a stock — or the entire market — takes a dive, it may be time to reassess your investments. You can't consider new alternatives if you allow the past to control your future.

Take Advantage of Timely Opportunities

Powerful outside forces can impact our lives. Wars, earthquakes, floods and hurricanes can create unplanned events of disastrous proportions. Sometimes they also create valuable — though unplanned — learning experiences. Other powerful outside forces are caused by changes in laws and customs. An opportunity that was unavailable earlier may suddenly become available because of a change in the law or the appropriation of money. The alert career seeker must pay attention to these changing circumstances and act promptly to take advantage of them. The case of James Montoya illustrates this point.

Born in the Right Year

My world in San Jose was self-contained — very local and very Latino working class. My father was a postal worker and my mother a part-time housekeeper. Neither had finished high school, but that did not keep me from understanding at an early age that they were both very, very smart; just not formally "educated." My sister also inherited their "smarts."

I often wonder what my sister's life would be like now if she had been presented with the same opportunities I was in 1971 through "affirmative action." Sylvia is two years older than I am. I earned As in physiology, the rigorous science course at Lincoln High School in San Jose. She earned A+s and won the top science award. Sylvia went on to San Jose State while working the night shift at the post office. I will never forget how happy she was for me when I woke her up to show her my admission letter from Stanford. She smiled and encouraged me to "go away from home" rather than to the local university. I share this moment to demonstrate how quickly the world changed for successful minority high school students, 1969 versus 1971. My sister eventually joined the U.S. Air Force, married, raised two daughters and earned her degree in business administration at Boise State University at age forty-one. She is still slightly intimidated by my world; a world she missed being a part of by literally two years.

The availability of affirmative action programs in 1971 gave James an opportunity that his equally talented sister did not have in 1969. James saw the opportunity, applied to Stanford and was accepted. Possibly Sylvia would have been accepted in 1969 too, but she did not get the encouragement to apply that affirmative action law made available. James was not only born in the right year to take advantage of his opportunity, he was alert to it and took the appropriate action. What opportunities are available to you this year that might not have been available a few years (or even a few days) ago? How are you staying alert to changing circumstances? What actions could you take now to capitalize on new laws, new appropriations, new businesses, or new educational programs?

Stanford Report, October 28, 1998, p. 20. Reprinted by permission.

Always Do Your Best Work — It Pays Off Later

It is a reasonable expectation that hard work on a task should result in a good outcome — though the world is not always that fair. What is sometimes overlooked, however, is that hard work is recognized by others and can lead to unexpected benefits later.

Hard Work Pays Off in Unexpected Ways

I think that growing up poor has a lot to do with where I am today. As a child, it was frustrating to see all the awesome new toys on television but to know that my parents couldn't afford them for us. At first, it was also embarrassing to tell people that my parents couldn't read or speak in English. In fact, I was their interpreter at the doctor's office, grocery store, and restaurants. In time I recognized that despite the fact that at a young age it was difficult to be an interpreter for my parents, I was serving an important function for our family. I came to realize that hard work can pay off in unexpected ways. I learned that doing my best would provide me with the opportunity to both improve my situation and also make my family proud.

As a child, my younger siblings and I wanted to follow our father's footsteps in becoming a mechanic. Although we didn't know the physical labor involved or the type of training needed, we knew it was a job that paid the bills. In my culture, it is more valuable to help out with the family's finances than to go to college. Therefore, my parents insisted that I find a full time job, preferably as a mechanic, upon high school graduation. As I grew older, I realized that I wouldn't enjoy getting dirty and working under a car's hood all day. I knew that such a job paid the bills, but still didn't pay enough for my parents to live a very comfortable life. I wanted something to fulfill my financial needs and something where I wouldn't mind waking up in the morning and going to work. I wanted a job where I could afford to vacation for at least a week out of the year, and still have extra money to set aside for emergency spending.

Since I did not know what kind of job I wanted, I began to explore various jobs while in high school. When I was sixteen, I worked as an activity's assistant at a children's amusement park called Fairy Tale Town. Although I liked working with children, I wanted something more interesting, so I found a job as a preschool assistant. After working as a preschool assistant, I realized that working with children wasn't as fun as I had envisioned it, so I found a job as a cashier at a local supermarket. After working at more customer-related jobs, I realized that I wanted to attend college, but also recognized that it was important to continue working and gaining experience.

I believe that hard work pays off, and that opportunity will not come knocking on my door, and as a result, I tend to work towards many goals simultaneously. Most importantly, I don't like to invest all my eggs in one basket; rather I like to keep my options open. I find that when I stick to a plan, things don't always go as planned.

While in college, I got a job as a receptionist through one of my friends. I began networking and found out that one of our clients was looking for an intern for his company. At first, I was a bit reluctant to apply because I felt that I didn't have the skills needed for that position. However, I was encouraged to apply and reassured that as an intern, I would get to learn from square one. After accepting the internship position, I learned that they had a full-time position at one of their offices. Again, I was reluctant to apply because this would mean that I would have to relocate. In addition, the full-time position was not related to my internship; therefore, I felt that I wasn't qualified. After talking to my co-workers, they told me that I'd learned more than they expected me to learn, and with my learning speed, they felt I would succeed. With their encouragement, I applied, and got the position. Although I did not know what to expect, I went in with an open mind and willingness to learn. Never would I have imagined working as an application support representative for a billing and clinical software company.

Let's review what helped Jenny to succeed:
- She helped her family by serving as interpreter.
- She recognized the benefits of always doing your best work.
- She came to the realization that she did not want to follow in her father's footsteps since she did not enjoy the tasks associated with being a mechanic.
- She tried two different jobs working with children to determine what she liked and disliked.
- She tried out jobs as a cashier, in customer service, and as a receptionist in order to gain experience and learn about other opportunities.
- She overcame her reluctance to pursue an internship because she didn't yet possess all of the skills necessary to do the job.

Jenny grew up in poverty and at one time believed that she had limited career options. She was able to overcome obstacles by taking action, doing her best, and being open-minded as well as always willing to learn.

The Voice Was Familiar

It was my sophomore year and I was taking a heavy load in terms of course work. I wasn't doing particularly well in my Russian language class so I was trying to boost my GPA before report cards arrived at Mom and Dad's. I was enrolled in a biology course at the time and I knew that if I did really well on the final paper that I would get an A and redeem myself for my poor work in Russian.

I remember working very hard on that biology paper — researching, writing, and rewriting. The teaching assistant in the biology class was Nancy. I asked Nancy to read drafts of my paper several times. I got her advice on a variety of excruciating details. Nancy was kind enough to tolerate this kind of behavior. When the class ended, I got an A for all my efforts and my parents forgave me for the C+ in Russian.

But the story doesn't end there . . .

At the start of the next semester, I wanted to get some research experience so I started to look at postings in the Biology Department. I saw one and walked into the biology lab to get an application. I introduced myself, and one of the graduate students handed me an application. He told me to fill it out and place it in the pile of applications that was about four inches high. Looking at the stack and knowing I had zilch in terms of experience, I just took the application with me and left, knowing it was a lost cause.

When I got home, my mother told me that I had gotten a call from someone named Nancy and that she wanted me to help her in her research. I returned her call immediately. Nancy had overheard my voice and remembered me from last semester. She had dashed out of the lab trying to find me and offer me a job, but I had somehow disappeared.

Even though I had not turned in an application to be a research assistant, I got the job anyway because Nancy, whom I had bugged so much, just happened to be working in that lab and recognized my voice. I guess it was fate! At any rate, that first job experience with Nancy helped me get other research experience in biology, and eventually enabled me to get into graduate school.

Was it fate that got Janet that first research job? Janet may think so, but look at what she did:

- She worked very hard on that first term paper.
- She consulted with the class TA — Nancy — regularly.
- She was conscientious and persistent in "bugging" Nancy, in a way that led Nancy to admire her.
- She wrote an excellent paper.
- She looked for job prospects in the Biology Department.
- She walked into the lab and spoke to the other graduate assistant, asking for an application. (An element of luck was present in that Nancy "happened" to be nearby.)

Janet would never have received that telephone call if she had just waited at home for it. She probably made a mistake in not filling out the application, but her good work and initiative set the stage for luck to play its part.

Ask for What You Want

Some people work for years doing a fine job but get little recognition or appreciation. Some get burned out and want to try something else. And some find their work is so highly valued that their present boss doesn't want to lose them.

Inertia can hold you in a position where you no longer want to be. Only you can take the action needed to change. No sense being shy about it — ask for what you want! Here's what Wu-Ki did.

"Why Not Just Ask?"

I was working at Macy's as a mid-level store executive. I hated my job and saw no prospects but more of the same. I had majored in history in college and realized that the computer was the key to increased productivity now just as the steam engine was in the nineteenth century. I had tried to get a computer job, but I didn't know enough to "fake" an interview.

One day I was having lunch with my fiancée (now my wife) and she said, "Why don't you just go to the Macy's computer department and ask them for a job?" I had never thought of such a simple direct approach.

So I went to talk to the manager and in five minutes I had the job. There was some hassle about the transfer within Macy's, but it got worked out.

After I learned what to do, I really liked my job, and it was a great career move.

When Desperate, Remember Those You've Helped

Sometimes it is necessary to call attention to yourself, impress other people, be persistent and maintain all your contacts. In the past you probably have helped other people in one way or another. They will remember your kindness and may well be inclined to return the favor. Don't be bashful about asking.

Cash in Your Chits

I am a single mom and lawyer who worked three years in Paris and then returned and worked mainly in legal software. I left my last job because a psychopath working there was harassing me. I was fairly distressed at the thought of having to explain why I left my last job so quickly. I was worried

I wouldn't be able to find work at my level that wouldn't involve a commute or long hours.

I interviewed with eight companies and had multiple interviews with some of them. I attended three career fairs and had exploratory interviews with a number of people. All of this interviewing, although tiring and sometimes discouraging, gave me the practice I needed to impress people quickly with my major strengths.

Although I obtained interviews through newspaper ads, internet ads and career fair contacts, the way I found this job was through the power of connections and timing. In my last job I hired an independent consultant named Ben to work on a software project. Later he formed a company of his own in the telecommunications industry, and I maintained contact with him. So when I started running low on leads in my job search, I figured Ben owed me a favor. I thought it was the time to call in my chit with him, so I phoned him to ask if he knew of anyone looking for a marketing professional. He told me that his own company was just about to launch a search for a marketing director, and I was able to persuade him to schedule me for an interview.

I had no experience with the telecommunications industry and knew that I would have to prove myself. Still, these guys hired me for who I was, not for the line-by-line on my resume (which they didn't even want to see) and that felt GREAT! I learned that I need to keep all my pots simmering because I never know which one will satisfy my appetite.

Don't Let Self-Doubt Keep You from Trying

It is normal to wonder whether you can handle a new situation. You've never dealt with a situation just like it before, so naturally you don't know whether you can handle it now. Self-doubt is a normal feeling, but self-doubt is not a reason to refrain from taking action.

Starting a New Life

In May 1996, Gwen crammed her belongings into her car, leaving behind her mother, stepfather, and a marriage that hadn't worked out. Leaving New York, she was drawn to sunny happy memories of having visited her father in California when she was ten. She planned to enroll in graduate school in English literature. She planned to be a professor. In her spare time, she'd write fiction — something she'd always done. Due to her previous experience, Gwen decided that she wasn't cut out for an office job. "Being an account executive didn't seem creative to me." On the other hand, her previous job at a major bookstore on the East Coast had intensified her passion for books.

When she landed in San Diego, she contacted her former boss, and thanks to his help she landed a job as an assistant manager at a local bookstore. The intent was to make a little money while she was getting settled. "The job was exciting, I was going back and forth between stores hiring and training staff, and overseeing renovations."

Four months later she had settled into a routine and grew restless. "I enjoyed being around books, but only because I liked to read and write. I didn't want to be an administrator with no time for my real interests."

It was too late to enroll in graduate school that semester, so Gwen began to look for another job. "I looked in the paper, sent my resume out to several newspapers, but nothing came of that. Then I saw an ad for a position in marketing at a company that manufactures organizers and agendas in Los Angeles. I thought it was the worst-case scenario, but I'll take a day trip to L.A. and chalk it up as an adventure."

She drove up for an interview two weeks later, full of doubt. To her surprise, she found that the place "felt like a perfect fit. The people were relaxed, and the place was fun and creative. And while the job I was applying for was administrative, I knew I might eventually get an opportunity to write."

One week later, Gwen was asked back for a second interview and was hired. Seven months later, one of the managers left. Gwen's workload doubled, and one of her responsibilities was to write press releases, copy for packages and catalogs, material for the Web, and time-management brochures. Not only did she love copywriting, she also showed a flair for it. Five months later she was promoted to Marketing Communication Specialist/Copywriter. "I can't believe I manage the copy team for a multimillion dollar company all by myself. I was lucky to get a chance to show my bosses I could write."

Mademoiselle, August 1998, pages 125–126. Reprinted by permission.

But was she just "lucky?" Let's look at the actions that Gwen took to create luck for herself:

- She relocated to start a new life.
- She contacted a former employer for help securing new employment.

- She made the most of every employment opportunity by giving her best effort.
- She was willing to change her employment plans.
- She was willing to change jobs, once she discovered that her job had become routine.
- She viewed the application process as an adventure, not a measure of her self-worth.
- She applied for a new job, despite having self-doubt.
- She took on new responsibilities at work when presented with an opportunity to do so.

Persist in the Face of Rejection

Persistence can be annoying to other people, but it can also pay big dividends. The story of Bob is a classic case.

Lack Experience? Go Get Some!

Although Bob had been accepted to Harvard Law School, he chose instead to pursue the field of journalism. He wanted very much to work at the *Washington Post*. The editor at the *Post* was not interested in hiring someone with so little experience, but Bob convinced him to take him on for two weeks at no pay just to see how he would do.

At the end of the two weeks, none of Bob's stories had been printed. The editor felt Bob was a bright man but lacked the skills to be a journalist. He told Bob that it would take too much energy to train him. He suggested that Bob should get some experience and come back in a year.

Bob did just that. He took a job with a competitor of the *Post*, and before long, began to jump on stories, beating-out the Post reporters. After a few months Bob started to call the *Post* again, but the editor would not take his calls. Bob found out the editor's home phone number where he called him early one Saturday morning. When the editor complained to his wife that he was tired of this young upstart pestering him, his wife responded, "Isn't that what you always say is the kind of person you want?"

The editor agreed, and he hired Bob, who had taken a gamble by calling the editor of the *Washington Post* on a Saturday morning. It might not have worked out as he hoped. He had sized up the editor as someone who valued aggressive reporters. Bob Woodward has gone on to become the world-famous journalist and author who broke the story of the Watergate scandal, leading to the resignation of President Richard Nixon. You need to assess each situation yourself to decide whether a bold gamble is worth the risk.

Consider Other Ways to Create Unplanned Events

The stories in this chapter illustrate just a few of the ways in which people have created their own beneficial unplanned events by taking action. Participants in a recent workshop in New Zealand have suggested a number of other actions — some of which are listed below. We have organized them in a way that may be useful to you.

Preparing for Action
- Commit your actions to paper and make a list of action steps.
- Take small steps to feel safe.
- Make arrangements so that you can attend the next club meeting, PTA meeting, etc.
- Say "yes," and then work out how you're going to do it.
- Tell yourself, "I'm going to do one thing differently today" and then do it.
- Think how your actions will benefit others, not just yourself.
- Investigate current problems in the workplace and come up with ideas for solving them.

Overcoming Barriers to Action
- See the humor in this sometimes ridiculous world of ours.
- Don't be put off by rejection — get up and try again.
- Realize that if your action fails, you are no worse off than if you did nothing.
- Learn how to manage stress — relax your mind and body.
- Celebrate your small successes.
- Participate in confidence-building exercises, such as accepting compliments gracefully.
- Stop making excuses for delaying action.
- Practice desired actions by role-playing first with supportive friends.

Taking Action I: Talk with All Kinds of People

- Network, socialize, build relationships.
- At every meeting or function, aim to speak to three new people.

THE FUSCO BROTHERS By J.C. Duffy

Discuss your career concerns with most everyone you meet.

- Find someone who is passionate about his or her job and ask questions about it.
- Talk to a friend about your career concerns.
- Talk about your career concerns with most everyone you meet.
- Talk to someone you would normally avoid because you feel intimidated.
- Talk to someone famous at a book signing or at other venues.

Taking Action II: Continue Learning

- Research areas of interest.
- Check out books from the library.
- Email well-known individuals with intriguing questions about their work.
- Take a personal development course, e.g., Toastmasters meeting, community college class.
- Surf the Internet to discover new information about a topic of interest.

Taking Action III: Try New Activities

- Take a different route home.
- Take up a new hobby or sport.
- Volunteer with an organization that intrigues you.
- At a party, pose challenging questions, e.g., "What would you do if you won the lottery?"
- Create an on-line chat group that's open to people with similar interests.
- Buy a guitar, rent a piano, or begin to learn some other musical instrument.

Taking Action IV: Involve Yourself in a Project

- Join a club, association or interest group.
- Help to organize an event.
- Put together a creative proposal aimed at solving a particular problem.
- Create your own business card.
- Seek a transitional job.
- Start experimenting by taking small steps in an area of interest.
- Produce a creative video or brochure to promote yourself.
- Start up a low risk business, e.g., dog walking.
- Offer to train/lecture/share knowledge.

Taking Action V: Create Your Own Career Luck

Here are some important tips you could have picked up from reading this chapter:

- Go one step at a time.
- Realize the future starts right now.
- Take advantage of timely opportunities.
- Always do your best work; it pays off later.
- Ask for what you want.
- When desperate, remember those you've helped.
- Don't let self-doubt keep you from trying.
- Persist in the face of rejection.
- Consider other illustrative actions for creating unplanned events.

Enough Talk About It — Time to Do It

Now is the time for *you* to take some action.

1. First make a wish about your career. Fill in the blanks to express your wish: "I wish that _____ would phone me and say to me,
   "_____
   _____"

2. If you do absolutely nothing, what is the probability that your wish will come true?
   ___ 0% ___ 25% ___ 50% ___ 75% ___ 100%

3. So let's take some action to increase the probability (no guarantees here!). Write down again the name of the person you want to call you: _____

4. Now find out that person's telephone number (be creative, use Directory Assistance, the name of the organization where that person works, a search engine on the Internet, someone who knows someone who knows someone who knows . . .). Write the phone number here: _____

5. Now dial the number.

6. If you reach the person, express in your own words the following idea: "Hello, Mr./Ms. _____, this is _____ from _____ and I'd like to help with the important

work you are doing on _____. I'm not selling anything except my abilities, and I'm not representing anyone except myself. I'd like to schedule a time to talk with you about ways I could help you. Would some time next _____day work for you?"

7. If you don't reach the person directly, leave a message and/or inquire about a convenient time to call back. Keep the initiative yourself — don't expect the person to call you back.

Making the Most of Happenstance

All too frequently people wait for an opportunity to knock on their door. Waiting doesn't work. We want you to do the knocking. You will quickly be surprised at how many opportunities you will discover. You don't even have to wait until you learn all the skills required for a new job before you apply, as you will learn in the next chapter.

Chapter 7

Go for the Job — Then Learn the Skills

Experience is a hard teacher because she gives the test first, the lesson afterwards.
— Vernon Sanders Law

Teachers open the door, but you must enter by yourself.
— Chinese proverb

Education is not the filling of a pail, but the lighting of a fire.
— William Butler Yeats

Many people think they should get paid for what they know. It's what you can do for me with what you know that brings value.
— Napoleon Hill

One of the big myths of our time is that you should be trained to perform a specific occupation before becoming employed in it. While there are some jobs which require specific educational preparation, you never learn all that you need to know from that initial training. The most valuable lessons are usually learned on the job.

One woman who rose through a series of jobs in various companies to become vice president of a major publishing company was quoted as saying, "I never accepted a job that I knew how to do."

HERMAN

"Hey, Mom. I got that job. Get over here
quick and show me what to do."

Reprinted with Permission of Newspaper Enterprise Association, Inc.

You don't need all the skills to apply —
you can learn on the job.

She convinced each employer that she could learn the new job. After
she got the job, she learned how to do it.

The best jobs used to be those where an employer guaranteed
you lifelong employment. Your expectation was that job security
was just another part of the employment package, right there with a
competitive salary and a solid benefits package. Your employer
would hire you right out of school and "take care of you," much like
a loving parent.

That expectation of permanent job security may never have been realistic, but now it is even less so. Fast-moving technological developments create rapid changes in job opportunities.

Never Complete Your Education

If you can't rely on the traditional form of job security anymore, is there anything else that you can rely on to build security? You'll be happy to know that there is, and it's called "lifelong learning."

"Hey," you may be thinking, "I've already finished my education."

Don't ever think that you have completed your education, no matter how much education you have. Learning goes on all the time, but you may or may not be learning anything useful.

If you shudder at the thought of going back to school, you shouldn't be alarmed. Learning can take place anywhere — outside a classroom, as well as in one. Don't think you necessarily need to return to school. Some people have had negative experiences in school, and want no more of that treatment. Fortunately you can learn anywhere. Everywhere you go, everyone you meet, and everything you read or hear or experience contributes to your learning. And you might be surprised to find how much fun it is to participate in a class when everyone there really wants to learn for the sake of learning, not just to get a grade (e.g., online, adult education, community college evening classes, workshops, seminars . . .).

Keep Learning Practical Skills to Deal with Poverty

The following story by Beverly Potter describes some of the ways she was able to deal with tragedy and poverty.

> My father, an Air Force jet pilot, died in a plane crash when I was a twelve-year-old child. With my father being in the military, we moved frequently. When in the second grade, for example, I went to five different schools. I always went to "town" schools, which more often than not were pretty poor, so I fell further and further behind over the years. By the eighth grade I was reading the second grade reader in the back of the room with the other remedial students.

Between my academic challenges and difficult economic situation, going to college didn't seem too likely. So imagine my surprise when I was accepted by Syracuse University — the only school I'd applied to. I was thrilled until one of the "popular" girls told me "they accept a lot of students to give them a chance, but most don't make it and are sent home after the first semester."

I was terrified when I arrived at the dorm in the fall. I was being given *one shot* at college. I *had* to make it or I was out! I had to study way more than others, of course. I carefully read every assignment, while underlining. I transcribed the underlined sections into a notebook. I stayed up almost all night memorizing before the exam. My efforts paid off. I made it through the semester!

Because my father had died on duty, I was a "war orphan" and received a small educational benefit similar to the GI Bill. It was hardly enough to pay for tuition, room and board, books, and such. The expense was a strain on my mother, who had never worked before and who wasn't all that thrilled that I was getting to go to college when she hadn't. So I left Syracuse and made my way to San Francisco State.

There I was in San Francisco and had to pay for rent, utilities, food, clothes, tuition, transportation to school, books, and everything else I needed. I didn't feel oppressed, however, because I had my own money and I was free! I never spent a penny on anything that was not a necessity. I never allowed myself even a soft drink. While my academic skills needed a lot of work, I had to be resourceful — very resourceful.

I had a can-do attitude, which I got from my father. He was a bad reader, too — though much worse than I was. He had dropped out of high school to go to cadet school. He was considered to be a mechanical genius, as was my grandfather, who had invented and built an actual car, circa 1930. My father was constantly taking cars and their engines apart, and then putting them back together. When I was six, instead of playing, I had to work on my bike when my father worked on the car.

While my father tinkered I made a make-shift doll bed that rocked on two half-round blocks of wood I'd found in a huge container of scrap wood. I had to stand on tip-toes to reach into it. Periodically, I was called over to worm my way into some horribly awkward spot to hold a bolt tight with a wrench so my dad could tighten the nut. He was my teacher.

I was resourceful, which made up for not having enough money. Someone "turned me on" to a Goodwill Store where I bought the cheapest stuff and refurbished it, like a chair for twenty-five cents that needed re-gluing. I had taken a sewing class in high school and was good at it. I could sew anything and made all of my clothes. But I was too poor to afford to buy cloth — so I used old curtains I bought at the Goodwill. One time I made a wonderful suit-type jacket out of old jeans I bought for a few dollars. Another time I bought dyed pelts at a local tannery, which I made into a leather dress I wore to my screening interview when applying for graduate school. When asked about the dress, I explained. They were impressed and I was accepted. I don't know if the leather dress helped — but it didn't hurt!

I didn't stop at making my clothes and upholstering my furniture, I made all of my dishes, too. I learned how to use a potter's wheel to "throw" pots and dishes. This was great because clay was cheap. Soon every surface in my apartment was crammed with all kinds of pots and containers. Christmas gifts for all. And at no additional cost!!! Slapping clay around has a certain satisfaction and throwing pots on a spinning wheel is hypnotic, so "potting" became a restorative benefit for my health.

I wanted nice things. I merely had to make them myself. I took a class at the craft center to learn lost-wax casting, where the piece is first carved out of wax, which is set into plaster, and then burnt out in a kiln. I used discarded dental tools to carve the wax and an old silver spoon that I melted to create the piece. Voila!!! Whenever I wanted or needed something I couldn't afford, I learned how to make it. I even repaired my car.

I had similar experiences with construction. A boyfriend and I ripped apart a dilapidated old house he bought in San Francisco with his meager inheritance. While living there, we demolished the back of the house, along with the bathroom. We built a foundation and a two story addition with a deck on top — all while the house sat on jacks. Though we broke up, I learned a lot — quite a lot — about construction.

My collection of skills served me well. I cultivated a can-do attitude, which enabled me to take on all manner of projects that "I didn't know how to do." No problem; I quickly learned how! Eventually, I purchased a rental property. There were repairs to do and improvements to make with a modest budget. No matter, I was ready with my toolbox and ladder. I found a broken up red sidewalk that someone had dumped into an empty lot. Little by little, I loaded it up in my old car, carting it to my house where I used it to create a patio. Another time, I bought an old fence for only five dollars and hired an old boyfriend-turned-carpenter to create a rustic–looking yard closet. When I couldn't fix something, I knew enough to ask the right questions to avoid being victimized by unscrupulous operators.

My can-do approach was not restricted to crafts and construction. I took a college-level tax preparer class so I could do my taxes, which are complicated because of my rental properties and other investments. By doing my own taxes I am better able to control my finances and I am better able to create "financials" that banks like enough to give me loans to do a remodel or buy a new building.

So resourcefulness, which is mostly attitude — I "can-do" that! — made up for a small budget and academic difficulties. Believing that I could accomplish what I set out to do enabled me to overcome my earlier learning deficits. Employing my numerous practical and financial skills, over time I've been able to build a rental property business sufficient enough that I no longer must scrimp. I still do save, however, which is another skill — an important skill.

Bev had a can-do attitude that enabled her to learn a variety of practical skills. She learned how to:
- Achieve academic success by studying intensively
- Scrimp by using her limited income for only the most vital expenses
- Use tools
- Repair houses with her construction skills
- Make her own pots and dishes out of clay
- Cut hair
- Sew clothes
- Find necessities at second-hand stores
- Compute her own income taxes
- Save money by putting it into a bank, not by buying discounted luxuries
- Acquire real estate at bargain prices
- Think positively about how her bargaining was making her feel rich

Beverly now owns a publishing company, Ronin Publishing, and publishes books about a variety of useful subjects.

Claiming Competence Based on Future Learning

Knowing that you can learn is an important qualification in itself. You don't necessarily have to know how to do a job *now* in order to claim that you can indeed do it, as Nikolai's story illustrates.

"Yes, I Can!"

Nikolai arrived in the United States from Eastern Europe with his wife and two small children. Despite the fact that Nikolai spoke three languages (Russian, German, and Polish), neither he nor his wife spoke any English. He came to the United States as a refugee and felt fortunate to have located a distant cousin who sponsored him and his family. They were able to find temporary housing living in the apartment building owned by the cousin, and Nikolai began picking up English words immediately. He needed work to support his family, but with his lack of formal education and his English language deficiency, he worried about his job prospects in the United States.

A neighbor in the building told him that jobs were frequently posted on a nearby bulletin board. Nikolai went with an acquaintance who read and spoke both Russian and English to find the bulletin board and see what was available. He listened intently as several job announcements were read to him by the acquaintance. One particular listing caught his attention. A nearby military base was advertising for barbers. What made the announcement most intriguing to Nikolai was the fact that the announcement included the words "license not required." Nikolai had never cut anyone's hair, but he remembered watching sailors give each other haircuts. It seemed pretty easy since the haircuts all looked about the same — just cut off all the hair. He spent the evening practicing short sentences that he had learned from his cousin that afternoon, including "Hello, it's nice to meet you" and "Yes, I can."

The next day Nikolai took the first bus out to the base. After showing the ad to an MP at the front gate, he received a map of directions to the barber shop. After an exchange of greetings, the barber shop manager asked Nikolai, "Can you give someone a haircut?"

"Yes," Nikolai answered, "I can. Cut it all off!"

Not only did Nikolai get the job, but within just two years, he had learned to do the job so well that he became the manager of the barber shop. He was the one who now did all of the hiring. His English language skills had improved immensely, and he was often invited over to the top officers' homes for dinner. He also acquired a love for country music, since many of the base personnel were from southern states, and the music played constantly in the shop.

When Nikolai was asked, "Can you give someone a haircut?" he could have truthfully answered, "I don't know. I've never done it before." Such an admission would probably have cost him the job. Instead he confidently asserted, "Yes, I can," and proved it to be true by subsequently learning how to cut hair. The fact that he had observed how to give a proper military haircut before arriving in the United States certainly worked in his favor when he told the manager "Cut it all off!"

To be realistic, there are jobs — brain surgeon and airplane pilot come to mind — for which you obviously need specific training so you don't endanger the lives of other people or yourself. But you have to start somewhere and must have the confidence that you can learn the necessary skills. Only in rare instances do you need to have all of the job competencies in advance.

Make Every Job a Learning Experience

You can start out in one direction, find your path blocked by conditions beyond your control, and then expand your interests in another direction. Maria's story illustrates this point.

Appraising Teaching in a Down Market

I was pursuing my teaching credential after I had been out of school for two years, With a degree in marketing, I had worked for an advertising agency and taught English in Argentina. I needed a part-time job while working on my credential, and a friend suggested I go to work for the appraisal firm she worked for. The job was to estimate how much a home or other property was worth. The boss hired me on my friend's recommendation and I started working part-time and learning the appraisal business. Concurrently I completed my teaching credential program and student teaching. Unfortunately it was during a time when teachers were being laid off. I could not find a full-time teaching position. I did some substitute teaching part-time and continued at the growing appraisal company.

As the company grew, I assumed more responsibility, first as a manager, then a director, and ultimately as vice president of a real estate finance company.

Maria started out wanting to be a teacher but ended up as an executive in a real estate finance company. Frustrated by the economic woes of the time in the teaching profession, and unable to find a teaching position, she continued her part-time work in the real estate appraisal business. She continued learning on the job, and the knowledge she acquired enabled her to advance despite her lack of formal training in the real estate business.

Everyone Is Your Teacher

Geoff was another who discovered that he did not need to learn only from credentialed teachers. Everyone with whom you come in contact can teach you something. Geoff discovered this to his great benefit.

Building Skills in Math

Between college graduation in biology and active military service, I worked as an assistant (a "gofer") for a construction superintendent. His formal education had ended in the sixth grade. In the few months that I worked for him he taught me more math than I had been able to learn in sixteen years of formal schooling. After I got out of the military I went back to school. The math that I learned from that construction superintendent provided me with the skills and self-confidence that I needed to advance in the field of engineering.

Use the Skills Learned in One Job to Qualify for the Next

Some learning experiences are planned and sponsored by employers. Others are acquired incidentally as a result of contacts and experiences along the way. With an open mind and a willingness to learn, Victoria found herself following an unexpected but satisfying path.

Jacuzzi Jumpstarts Job Search

When I moved to the United States from England, I could not find anyone who would employ me. To kill time and get into shape I joined a health club.

One day I struck up a conversation with another lady whilst wallowing in the Jacuzzi. She had just been offered work at a bank. She said they needed staff and were willing to train. She gave me the name of the person doing the hiring.

I had never done any work remotely similar to work in the banking industry. I applied and got a starting position on probation.

Within three months I was promoted to a permanent position. I worked at that bank for two-and-a-half years, during which time I learned accounting skills — just what I needed when I applied for and obtained another position with a high-tech company. I worked for a startup company doing online accounting on their web site. There I learned HTML, and now I am employed as an HTML production specialist.

Don't Underestimate Your Skills

When employers advertise a position opening, they frequently list a number of skills they want an applicant to have. This is the employer's wish list. However, just because you don't have every skill on the list is no reason not to apply. The employer basically is looking for someone who can help get the work done.

If you are friendly, can communicate with other people and are willing to learn, you already have the most important qualifications that most employers want. You don't need to know exactly how to do the job before you start. Employers expect you to learn on the job. They want you to learn. They want to teach you so you will do the job the way they prefer. What you have to provide is the eagerness to learn.

Not Perfect — But Better Than Your Average Bear

When I was in high school, I refused to learn keyboarding — thinking with my sixteen-year-old macho mind that only girls needed to know how to type. On my first day on the job in the newsroom of a major television station, I was taken to a desk with a computer and asked to type up a story from notes. As I began to type my first story using my hunt-and-peck method, my face reddened and I broke into a sweat as others noticed that I did not know how to do touch-typing.

Then I began to look around the room as I continued to work. Two of the news anchors were typing stories, and the station's star reporter was also typing a story. All three of them were also using the hunt-and-peck system, but they were pecking with only one finger of each hand. I knew I had them beat because I could use three fingers on each hand!

I continued working for that TV station for the next fourteen years.

Learn What You Enjoy from Your Own Experience

Your own personal experience gives you insights into what you really enjoy doing. It is indeed amazing that different people learn to enjoy different kinds of activities. Imagine how impossible the world would be if everyone wanted to be an accountant and no one wanted to be a teacher or a miner or a mechanic. Interest inventories can give you hints about what kinds of work you might enjoy, but only your own personal experience can convince you, as Stephanie's story illustrates.

Lesson from a Family Tragedy

I had majored in sociology in college because I wanted to help people. After graduating from college, however, I somehow found myself working in a corporate information technology job I didn't like. Several of my co-workers were getting downsized. I remember a co-worker telling me that it's good to have a backup plan. I decided that at some point I should take some classes learning things that I really liked.

At about this time, my mother had a stroke. I was able to watch and actually help the therapists who were assisting my mother. I learned how to move her and help her to exercise. Surprisingly, I found that I enjoyed these activities, as well as helping my mother, a lot more than my technology job. I also found it to be much closer in spirit to my college work in sociology.

I decided that a physical therapy degree would take me longer than I wanted to spend, so I went to school for massage therapy and haven't looked back since.

Stephanie's experience shows how even a tragically unexpected event, a family member's serious illness, can change a person's life in surprising ways. Stephanie found that her corporate job did not have the security that she had expected. At the same time she came to realize that it is important to consider "things I really liked" (i.e., "to help people"). She also discovered the importance of becoming flexible. When she found out that a physical therapy degree didn't fit her time frame for a career transition, she pursued a related area (massage therapy), and as she glowingly says now, "I haven't looked back since."

Give Yourself a Promotion

Many people want to advance through the ranks in the business or profession they have entered. A common strategy is to do good work and hope that it will be recognized and rewarded. Unfortunately, it does not always work out that way. In such cases it is important for the employee to take the initiative, as we see here in Paige's story.

A Legal Proposal

I started as a temporary paralegal in a law firm. They liked my work so much they offered me a permanent position. What I really wanted to do was enhance my skills in management.

When they offered me the job I wrote them a proposal as to what my job should be. Yes, I was willing to do paralegal work but I also wanted to be the legal manager.

They accepted my proposal. I worked with them for four years, acquired many new skills, and left to start a new career.

Paige's story provides proof that you can take advantage of a humble beginning if you do a good job. For many people, getting the offer of permanent employment would be enough. Paige was different. She wanted to learn more and enhance her skills. What did she have to lose by proposing more for herself and her employer? She took the initiative and wrote her own job description. Her proven track record and assertiveness led her beyond her own expectations.

Treat Obstacles to Learning as Challenges

While learning takes place all the time, you may not necessarily be in a position to learn what you want to learn in the way you prefer.

Gwen seemed to learn best by immersing herself in a culture and a job. She eventually pursued a more conventional way of learning, and found that had benefits she hadn't imagined.

"Why Not Spain?"

I was a pre-med student in college and wanted to spend my junior year abroad. I loved the Spanish language and my college teacher suggested going to Seville, Spain. I thought to myself, "Why not?"

I loved my junior year experience there so much that, after graduating the following year with a degree in Spanish literature, I decided to return to Spain. Little did I know at the time that I would be spending the next six years overseas. I taught English for two years there but became bored and wanted to try something else. But not being a Spaniard meant it was nearly impossible to get another job there.

So I looked into graduate programs and found an international MBA program in Barcelona. I went there for two years, worked at a biotech company for a year, and then was offered a job at the age of twenty-seven to open an investment promotion office in Barcelona run by an American company with headquarters in San Francisco. I moved on, and now work independently as an international marketing consultant.

When Gwen's teacher suggested spending her junior year abroad, Gwen was optimistic and asked "Why not?" In addition to being optimistic, Gwen also didn't let barriers get in her way. Although she found it difficult to get a new job because she was a foreigner, she discovered that there was another way for her to learn and still remain in Spain. She was able to attend graduate school, get an MBA degree, and create a new career direction in international business.

As you continue your learning, keep these points in mind:
- Never "complete" your education.
- Make every job a learning experience.
- Use the skills learned in one job to qualify for the next.
- Don't underestimate your skills.
- Learn what you enjoy from your own experience.
- Give yourself a promotion.
- Treat obstacles to learning as challenges.

Become a Lifelong Learner

Is there something that you have always wanted to explore and yet never found the time? It can help to start with a hobby that intrigues you, even one that seems to have no practical benefits. You will probably wish that you had not waited so long.

As you can tell from the stories in this chapter, it's never too late to have new learning experiences. We invite you to take a few minutes now to consider lifelong learning by answering the following questions:

1. What is one thing you would most like to learn?
   ___ How to do basic maintenance on your car (or appliances, or _____)
   ___ How to play tennis (or other sport: _____)
   ___ How to write a novel (or poetry, short stories)
   ___ How to converse in Spanish (or other language _____)
   ___ The history of the French revolution (or other event: _____)
   ___ How to refinish furniture
   ___ How to start your own business
   ___ How to play the piano (or other instrument: _____)
   ___ How to become a better public speaker
   ___ Other: _____

2. What's stopping you from learning what you would like to learn?
   ___ Not enough time
   ___ I don't know who could teach me
   ___ It would cost me too much
   ___ Other: _____

3. How about a friendly challenge to your reasons?
   Everyone has the same twenty-four hours every day. You get to choose how to use them. What hours could you make available?
   _____
   What would you need to do to find a teacher? _____
   _____
   ___ Could you teach yourself?
   ___ Could you find other interested people on the Internet?
   ___ Could you read a book on the subject?

How much exactly would it cost? _____
___ Is there a less expensive method of learning?
How could you start small initially? _____
_____

4. Think about one of the most enjoyable learning experiences that you ever had. What was it that made it so enjoyable?
___ I received individual attention
___ The teacher was dynamic and interesting
___ I learned it by myself
___ I learned as part of a team
___ I was able to put it to use right away in my life
___ Other: _____

5. What part of the learning activity do you personally find most helpful?
___ Hearing someone else describe it
___ Watching someone else do it
___ Doing it myself with someone guiding me
___ Doing it myself with no one else around
___ Other: _____

6. In what kind of setting do you most enjoy learning?
___ At home
___ At a library
___ Online (Internet)
___ In a classroom
___ On board a cruise ship
___ One-on-one with a teacher/coach
___ Through travel
___ By reading a book or manual
___ Other: _____

7. What are you going to do now to enhance your learning?
___ Nothing
___ I'm going to ask someone for advice on how best to begin
___ I'm going to take some action
___ Other: _____

8. When are you going to take the first step?
   ___ Right this minute
   ___ Within the next hour
   ___ Sometime today
   ___ Tomorrow
   ___ Other: _____

Making the Most of Happenstance

The world of work is no place to be bashful about your qualifications. If you don't know how to do something now, you can always learn. And learning need not be distasteful — you can have fun learning new skills. Like Geoff and Victoria and Stephanie and the others whose stories you read in this chapter, you will be learning new skills throughout your life. It's never too late to start learning, and you can enrich your whole life — not merely enhance your career.

Chapter 8

Enjoy Yourself — The Good Life Is a Balanced Life

Every moment is the chance of a lifetime.
— Pir Vilayat

The most successful people are those who do all year long what they would otherwise do on their summer vacation.
— Mark Twain

You get treated in life the way you teach people to treat you.
— Wayne Dyer

No one can make you feel inferior without your permission.
— Eleanor Roosevelt

This whole book concerns ways you can create a satisfying life for yourself, but so far we have been concentrating on only one part of life: your career. Certainly your main job requires many of the 168 hours in your week, but not all of them. In addition to eating and sleeping, you probably spend other important chunks of time devoted to relationships, family, sports, hobbies, education, daily chores, care-giving, exercise, travel, entertainment, part-time work, volunteer work, and spiritual concerns. The good life requires some balance.

Each of us gets to choose how to distribute the twenty-four hours in every day. And we all make unique choices. No one formula works for everyone. What's more, the choices you make today do not necessarily commit you to making the identical choices tomorrow.

Throughout this book, we've been pointing out how creating luck can help you build a satisfying career. In this chapter, we want to remind you that the same principles apply to all aspects of your life. For example, if you've been getting your exercise by jogging and find the process incredibly boring, try something else — tennis, golf, curling, ice skating, rollerblading, weight-lifting, riding a scooter, swimming. Talk with your friends and acquaintances about what they do. Get some new ideas. Make some mistakes. Try out some new alternatives and see what pleases you. Don't stay stuck in an exercise rut any more than you would a career rut.

Most of us with full-time jobs have to sandwich in these other activities around our working hours. If you don't have a full-time job and don't want one, you have more time to try out the same wealth of alternatives.

Sometimes, unplanned events lead people to quit working full-time — voluntarily or involuntarily:

- winning the lottery
- becoming rich through good stock investments
- receiving a substantial inheritance
- accepting a buy-out offer from your employer
- wanting to try something new and intriguing
- getting fired or laid off
- experiencing burnout
- becoming sick or disabled
- reaching mandatory retirement age
- passing peak physical ability (for athletes)

Regardless of the reason, you are still the one to call the shots about how you spend your time.

If you (like most of us) need paid employment, the first seven chapters of this book point out actions you can take to obtain a new job. If you are looking to enrich your life in other ways, or if your financial needs don't depend on earned income (e.g., you have insurance, independent wealth, Social Security, investments, pensions, royalties, legal settlements, inheritance, annuities, SSI, etc.), then this chapter has some good ideas for you to consider.

The answer to the question: "What do I do next?" still has to do with trying out new and intriguing activities. Whether you are twenty-one, fifty-one, or eighty-one, it's never too late to create a satisfying life for yourself. We will provide you with a few specific examples in this chapter.

Put Yourself in Charge of Creating a Satisfying Life

The reason people want to find the "one best occupation" is because they see it as leading to a satisfying life. No one can quarrel with that goal — a satisfying life — but one might quarrel with the assumption that there is only one best occupation that will achieve it. Life is not that simple. Work is part of life, but it is far from all of life. Being a member of a particular occupation does not guarantee a satisfying life. There are unhappy folks in every field of endeavor — doctors, used car salespersons, lawyers, mechanics, nurses, investment bankers, teachers. No one job can meet all our needs and interests. We change and grow through the years. Our jobs may change too, but not necessarily in ways compatible with our own developing preferences.

Good relationships are another important part of a satisfying life, and Karen's story illustrates how work and love are interrelated.

Going for the Ride of Your Life!

During one summer I was working in a restaurant to supplement my teaching income. One day, a man came into the restaurant, we began talking and found quickly that we were attracted to each other. He told me that he owned a motorcycle. I said that I had always wanted to ride on the back of a motorcycle and had never had the opportunity. He immediately picked up my hint and offered to take me for a ride.

Once we started dating, he introduced me to some old family friends of his. One of these friends worked at the local school's district office and another as a dean at a nearby university. Both of these people, upon hearing of my interests, encouraged me to apply to their organizations. Within six weeks of beginning to date this man, I had changed employers and entered graduate school.

Reprinted with Permission of United Feature Syndicate, Inc.

No matter how bad it gets, you can still create new opportunities.

This man is now my husband and continues to encourage me to follow my dreams. Imagine how different my life would have been had I failed to express my interest in riding on a motorcycle!

We are certainly not advocating that you ride on strangers' motorcycles! Karen, however, identified desirable qualities in the man she met, expressed her interest in his interests, and the resulting relationship led to a new job, graduate school and a husband. None of this could have been predicted, but Karen's initiative in making the most of a chance meeting enabled it to happen.

Everyone you meet is a stranger at first. Some who were strangers become your best friends. Most you never see again. However, you have considerable power to influence which of them become your friends and which do not. Just one person can make a big difference in your satisfaction with life. You want to exercise good judgment in making your choices. Some strangers should be avoided, of course, but Karen's choice worked out better than she could have imagined.

Learn Through Taking Up a Hobby

The benefits of learning need not be job related. Important as a satisfying job may be, life's joys include much more. Almost everyone finds other activities that enhance their enjoyment of life, but some postpone taking action until an event propels them into making a move, as we see in Justin's story.

The Procrastinating Musician

Since I was a small child, I always loved the sound of the guitar, especially the electric guitar. I loved the way rock and jazz guitarists could create different sounds, textures, and emotions through their playing. I always promised myself I would one day learn how to play. But somehow I "never got around to it." There never seemed to be enough time to learn. It didn't happen in high school, it didn't happen in college, and graduate school led to a career that consumed most of my time. The time that was left was for family and friends, and sometimes the occasional trip to the record store to buy a CD. For years, the best I could do was to be an active listener.

Then one day while shopping, my wife and I quite unexpectedly saw a combination electric guitar and amplifier for sale on the shelf in a discount store where we usually only buy bottled water and laundry detergent. She insisted on buying it for me because she had heard too many times about my unfulfilled passion. I agreed with her: now was the time.

Almost immediately, I found a private teacher at a local music store and started taking lessons. My study of the guitar has brought me all of the things that new learning can bring, including excitement, frustration, joy, and a true sense of accomplishment. I find that I love learning something new, even if it's pretty challenging.

Many people find that they have put a hobby or interest on the backburner for years. For Justin, it was learning how to play guitar. At first it may have seemed that playing the guitar had no practical benefit for Justin. He was wrong. Justin quickly discovered that seriously exploring guitar brought him "excitement, challenge, frustration, joy, and a sense of accomplishment."

Every Job Is about Helping Others

When you stop to think about it, every job in the world is concerned with helping other people. Bus drivers, accountants, artists, politicians, carpenters, broadcasters, teachers, and every other occupation — directly or indirectly — is of help to other people. One person pays for help, another provides a service or product that is of value to that customer.

Most of us reach a point in life when we have some measure of financial security and no longer need to work for income. Yet we can still gain satisfaction as we find other ways to help people without being paid for it.

Learning New Ways to Help Others

It's a dream nearly all of us have had. Your financial situation is well under control when you end your paid career, and you can spend your time as you choose. You may have had fantasies about doing little or nothing — lying on the beach, sitting at home watching TV, shopping at the mall. In actuality, doing little or nothing is incredibly boring no matter what your age. Traveling is an option for people who have not traveled much during their careers, but after a while even the most ardent traveler becomes weary and wants to return home.

Among the many ways that you might want to consider spending your time, one popular option for helping others is temporary employment.

Take Temporary Employment

Temporary employment, when it's available, offers a number of benefits: you have choice in the type of work you do, you work only as many hours as you choose, and you get paid too. You might go into business for yourself, for example, and offer your services to likely prospects, or you can sign up with a temporary employment agency in your community. Agencies tend to specialize in particular types of work — medical, secretarial, construction, technical, accounting, dental or general labor.

Here's what Dave did.

"I Love Going to Work"

Dave feels like a new man. After twenty-six years as an engineer, he found himself, when his position was downsized, out of a job at the age of sixty.

"I tried retiring," he recounts. "But I found myself wandering around trying to find something to keep me busy. One day I surprised myself and decided to attend a job fair and left my newly updated resume with a few temporary agencies." Within four weeks Dave was working for a temporary agency specializing in people with technical experience. "I really love going to work," Dave says. He is using skills acquired in many years on the job as an engineer, but without the stress of managing. In addition to earning a decent salary, he takes time off whenever he needs to.

Let's review the actions that Dave took to create new opportunities for himself:
- He attended a job fair.
- He developed an updated resume.
- He was open-minded about work as a temporary employee, and accepted such a role.

- He did his best in his new job, so well in fact, that he is earning as much as he did in a full-time job.
- He learned that he was valued by his friends and family for who he is, not for his job title.
- He learned that everyone — including temporary workers — should be treated with dignity and respect.

Get Into Politics

Before you reject political activity prematurely, think about what is really involved. You can have an opportunity to influence the world in which you live. You could become a member of the school board, a county commissioner, a fund raiser or a campaign worker. Politics requires many different kinds of contributions, and it requires more people like you — honest, incorruptible and dedicated to the general welfare. A notable example of someone who made it big in one field before getting involved in politics is former U.S. Senator Bill Bradley.

From Basketball Star to Presidential Candidate

In his memoirs Bill Bradley wrote, "My mother always wanted me to be a success. My father always wanted me to be a gentleman. Neither wanted me to be a politician." Yet he did become a politician — and a good one at that. How did it happen?

His first political memory was of his father, a staunch Republican, denouncing the local Democratic kingpin. At five years of age he remembers his parents hosting a party on election night to celebrate the expected victory of Thomas Dewey over Harry Truman. As the election returns came in, the guests left in a somber mood.

In grade school he actively supported Eisenhower for President and "...wore a shirt full of Republican political buttons." His Aunt Elizabeth was a member of the school board but lost in her race to become county assessor despite Bill's participation in a sign-waving caravan.

He considered entering politics as a Princeton senior and asked his father for advice. He suggested that Bill consult the same Democratic kingpin he had earlier denounced. Bill did and learned, "If I wanted to get into politics, I had to start at the bottom."

Bill had become an outstanding basketball player at Princeton University and played for the United States in the 1964 Olympics where his team won the gold medal.

At first he rejected the idea of playing professional basketball, choosing instead to obtain a master's degree at Oxford University in economics, philosophy and politics. Eventually he succumbed to an offer from the Knicks to play professional basketball. He played for them for ten years, participating in his team's winning two NBA championships, and becoming a well-known basketball hero. During this time he made occasional appearances in support of various political candidates. He attended a dinner for the Chairman of the House Judiciary Committee, lobbied senators and testified before the Senate Judiciary Committee opposing basketball's exemption from the antitrust laws. His interest in and knowledge of politics was growing.

After retiring from the Knicks at age thirty-four, Bill could have lived a life of leisure on his savings from basketball. He had never been a big spender. Instead he heeded a call from the Democratic Party which sought to capitalize on Bill's name recognition.

Bill's first attempt to enter politics was unusually successful. He says he "started at the top" — contrary to the political advice he had received. He became the U.S. Senator from New Jersey in 1979. His eighteen years in the U.S. Senate earned him a reputation for integrity in his battles for civil rights and energy conservation. After much internal debate he agreed to enter the race to become the Democratic nominee for President of the United States. Although he was defeated by Al Gore in 2000, he remains a respected political figure as well as the author of three non-fiction books.

Note the actions that Bill Bradley took before "starting at the top":
- He listened to his father's denunciations of a politician.
- He observed his parents hosting a political celebration.
- He actively supported his aunt's political ambitions.
- He sought the advice of the county political kingpin.
- He obtained a master's degree in politics.
- He demonstrated his athletic excellence on the basketball court.
- He supported local political candidates.
- He attended a political dinner.

- He lobbied senators.
- He testified before the Senate Judiciary Committee.

When he ran his first race for the Senate, his actions had already prepared him for the political battles ahead. He had not really "started at the top."

Volunteer Doing Something You Enjoy

Almost every organization can use some free volunteer help. People have found satisfying activities by volunteering at places such as museums, schools, hospitals, social service organizations, political organizations and hobby clubs. You may want to apply a skill you learned in the past, or you could learn a brand new skill. Here's what Bill Schwartz did:

Providing Medical Services for the Poor

Two years before Dr. Bill Schwartz "retired" from his medical practice in Northern California, he had the idea that a medical clinic for the poor was a necessity for his community. He had been considering volunteering part-time to provide much needed medical care to poor families. He felt that without his medical practice he had the time to provide this type of service to the community. He thought it might be a good idea to talk with a few hospital administrators about establishing a free medical clinic for the poor. Nothing fancy, maybe even something right in the hospital with hours that served the working poor. Dr. Schwartz was told there would be problems with liability, facilities, and equipment. Although most people thought it might be a good idea to have such a clinic, it just wouldn't be an efficient way to operate. Dr. Schwartz disagreed. He contacted several like-minded doctors as well as administrators with a non-profit organization, Samaritan House, who were supportive.

That was during the early 1990s. Now Dr. Schwartz likes to think of the Samaritan House Clinic that he helped to create as a "model of inefficiency." The small facility is so heavily staffed that doctors can talk casually with patients. They have time to read medical journals or have casual discussions with each other. In other words, these retired doctors, who average seventy-four years of age, are practicing medicine like they thought they should have since medical school graduation. Through the clinic, these doctors, nurses, and staff of the Samaritan House Clinic in San Mateo have continued providing service to others.

Let's review what Dr. Schwartz did to help create the Samaritan House Clinic:

- He acted on his idea that serving others was a good way to spend his "retirement."
- He sought out and spoke with several hospital administrators about his idea for a free clinic and was not deterred because of their initial lack of encouragement.
- He contacted other physicians and received their support for his idea.
- He formed an alliance with colleagues with a similar mindset, including administrators outside of medicine.
- He helped to establish a non-traditional work environment for the clinic that many call ideal for a medical office.

You are wanted by more people than you can imagine — especially if you are willing to help them free of charge. You can take the initiative yourself if you know of people or organizations that could use your help. If you run short of ideas about local organizations, handy sources of information include the yellow pages in your telephone book and the classifieds in your local newspaper. Look under a heading such as "Social and Human Services for Individuals and Families" to find organizations that would be happy to have you help them.

Would you enjoy the work? You'll never know until you try it. The advantage of volunteering is that if you don't like it, you can always quit and try something else.

Go to School

It is sometimes said that education is wasted on the young, an idea that grows from awareness that older people can really appreciate educational opportunities. Mature adults don't have to worry about getting good grades — they go just to learn. You can study as little or as much as you choose. You get to interact with other people who are interested in the same topics you are. Most colleges and school districts have adult education or continuing education programs with a wide variety of course offerings. You can take as many or as few courses as you want.

Rose wanted to get a degree.

"Be All You Can Possibly Be!" (Even at Eighty-seven)*

The first day of school our professor introduced himself and challenged us to get to know someone we didn't already know. I stood up to look around when a gentle hand touched my shoulder. I turned around to find a wrinkled, little old lady beaming up at me with a smile that lit up her entire being. She said, "Hi handsome. My name is Rose. I'm eighty-seven years old. Can I give you a hug?"

I laughed and enthusiastically responded, "Of course you may!" and she gave me a giant squeeze. "Why are you in college at such a young, innocent age?" I asked. She jokingly replied, "I'm here to meet a rich husband, get married, have a couple of children, and then retire and travel."

"No, seriously," I remarked. I was curious what may have motivated her to be taking on this challenge at her age. "I always dreamed of having a college education and now I'm getting one!" she told me. After class we walked to the student union building and shared a chocolate milkshake. We became instant friends. Every day for the next three months we would leave class together and talk nonstop. I was always mesmerized listening to this "time machine" as she shared her wisdom and experience with me.

Over the course of the year, Rose became a campus icon and easily made friends wherever she went. She loved to dress up and she reveled in the attention bestowed upon her from the other students. She was living it up.

At the end of the semester we invited Rose to speak at our football banquet and I'll never forget what she taught us. She was introduced and stepped up to the podium. As she began to deliver her prepared speech, she dropped her three-by-five cards on the floor. Frustrated and a little embarrassed she leaned into the microphone and simply said, "I'm sorry I'm so jittery. I gave up beer for Lent and this whiskey is killing me! I'll never get my speech back in order so let me just tell you what I know."

---

* The story of "Rose," the eighty-seven-year-old college graduate, has been re-told and passed around on the Internet and elsewhere for several years. While it is believed to be true, we have been unable to document it or discover an original source. It may turn out to be an urban legend, but it's inspirational enough that we consider it worth repeating.

As we laughed she cleared her throat and began: "We do not stop playing because we are old; we grow old because we stop playing. There are only four secrets to staying young, being happy, and achieving success:

"You have to laugh and find humor every day.

"You've got to have a dream. When you lose your dreams, you die. We have so many people walking around who are dead and don't even know it!

"There is a huge difference between growing older and growing up. If you are nineteen years old and lie in bed for one full year and don't do one productive thing, you will turn twenty years old. If I am eighty-seven years old and stay in bed for a year and never do anything, I will turn eighty-eight. Anybody can grow older. That doesn't take any talent or ability. The idea is to grow up by always finding the opportunity in change.

"Have no regrets. The elderly usually don't have regrets for what we did, but rather for things we did not do. The only people who fear death are those with regrets."

She concluded her speech by courageously singing *The Rose*. She challenged each of us to study the lyrics and live them out in our daily lives. The song ends with these words:

remember in the winter
far beneath the bitter snows
lies the seed that with the sun's love
in the spring becomes the rose.

At the year's end Rose finished the college degree she had begun all those years ago.

One week after graduation Rose died peacefully in her sleep. Over two thousand college students attended her funeral in tribute to the wonderful woman who taught by example that it's never too late to be all you can possibly be!"

Recall these ways of being all that you can be:
- Put yourself in charge of creating a satisfying life.
- Learn through taking up a hobby.
- Take temporary employment.
- Get into politics.
- Volunteer doing something you enjoy.
- Go to school.

Now It's Time for You to Enjoy Yourself

1. Do you feel stuck now with a bad choice you made in the past?
   Yes ___ No ___

2. If "Yes," what can you do now to get unstuck?
   _____
   _____

3. How do circumstances differ now from those that existed when you started?
   _____
   _____

4. Given today's circumstances, what choices would you like to make?
   _____
   _____

5. What advice have you received from others?
   _____
   _____

6. How are you reacting to that advice?
   ___ I tend to accept it uncritically
   ___ I tend to react defensively
   ___ I take it into account as I make my own plans

7. What steps could you take to transform your present situation into one that would be more satisfying for you?
   _____
   _____

Making the Most of Happenstance

You want to create a new life for yourself, and you have seen how other people have done it. But it's only fair to point out that the task is not easy. You will run into obstacles — some that other people put in your way, and some that you create in your own mind. The next chapter will show you how positive beliefs can help you overcome obstacles that might be blocking your progress.

Chapter 9

Overcome Self-Sabotage

Be the change you wish to see in the world.
— Mahatma Gandhi

Wisdom is not so much knowing what you must do in the end as knowing what you must do next.
— Herbert Hoover

Whether you think you can or think you can't — you are right.
— Henry Ford

A candle loses nothing by lighting another candle.
— Erin Majors

The fundamental message of this book is that a satisfying career — and a satisfying life — is found through actively creating your own luck and making the most of new and unforeseen experiences.

We've encouraged you to explore lots of alternatives, to learn more about things that intrigue you, and to consider how you might be of service to others. Becoming actively involved in intriguing activities is the key. But how do you know what is going to be intriguing? How do you know what to explore? How do you know what to learn? How do you know what's important?

The answer to these questions is that *there is no way for you to know in advance.* You find out by *trying* a variety of activities. Some you will like, some you won't. Sure, spend more time engaged in the things you like, but *keep exploring alternatives.*

Can You Really Create Your Own Passion?

But how about the popular advice to "discover your inner passion"? Isn't that good advice? Perhaps, but the crucial question is, how do you make the discovery? We don't think that sitting and contemplating your navel is a constructive way to discover your passion. Passion is cultivated by participating with other people engaged in important projects.

How do you find an ideal job? The best way is to take the first job offer that exposes you to the most learning opportunities and then take advantage of every chance you get to learn new skills and develop new interests.

Sometimes you may just want a job — any job — now. This may be exactly what you need to do at the time — to keep a roof over your head, to keep you active, to offer work experience. Even an undesirable job can teach you some important lessons. If your job meets your interests, all the better. Even if your job is not ideal, you still want to do your best work because you're building a reputation for dependability. Many jobs that people consider ideal for themselves at the time start out unpaid, or requiring menial labor, or both. You have to start somewhere. You can't expect a high-paying, high-responsibility job at first. You have to "pay your dues" by showing that you can perform well. Oprah Winfrey, one of the most successful television personalities ever, started as a receptionist.

Overcoming Obstacles to Action

Since taking action is the key, why is it that some people find it difficult to do?

There are two kinds of obstacles that inhibit taking action: *external* and *internal*. Think you might like to be an airline pilot? You can't just crawl into the cockpit and take off. It takes years of training and experience to prepare for that demanding responsibility — and that training is expensive. You don't have much money? There's an example of an external obstacle.

If you qualify in other respects, you might let the military service train you as a pilot, thus overcoming one of the external obstacles.

However, you will eventually discover that piloting an aircraft entails taking risks — among them the physical risks to life and limb and the fear of humiliation should you flunk out of training. Afraid to take such risks? That fear is an example of an internal obstacle.

Develop Helpful Beliefs

Both external and internal obstacles can be overcome, but we usually have greater control over the obstacles within us, so that is the place to begin concentrating your efforts. One important step is to develop a set of positive beliefs that will help you take constructive actions. If you believe you will fail, chances are you will. If you believe you can succeed, your chances of success are immeasurably improved. So let's focus on some beliefs that can help you confront and overcome your internal obstacles.

• **Some work experience is better than no work experience.** Nate has just received a master's degree in sociology. He has applied for a number of jobs and has actually received three job offers in the past two months. However, he turned down all three offers. He said, "They were not offering me enough money. I spent two years getting a master's degree on top of my four years in college. I deserve a higher salary." Nate is still unemployed.

Nate is suffering from the mistaken belief that years of formal education *entitle* him to a high-paying job. Employers do not pay for past years of schooling; they pay for *what you can do* for them now. They look for evidence that you have performed valuable services for other people in the past, because that's likely to predict whether you can do something valuable now. If Nate had spent all his time in school, and gained little or no job experience, no employer is going to risk paying him a high starting salary. Nate would be well advised to accept a position that gives him a chance to learn some work skills and demonstrate his value. He can negotiate for a higher salary later — after he's proved himself.

• **You can change your career direction now regardless of what you have done in the past.** Keisha didn't know what she wanted to do after finishing college. Under some pressure from her parents, she applied to law school, was accepted, and hated it. The competitive atmosphere, the endless memorization of legal precedents, the nuances and technicalities, and the emphasis on money all depressed her. Still she stuck it out, finished law school and took a job in a small law firm. Not surprisingly, she hated her job. When a friend asked why she didn't quit, she replied, "I can't quit! I have too much invested. I invested four years in college, three years in law school, and now I have three years' experience as a lawyer. I can't throw that all away."

Keisha's mistaken belief is that prior training and experience is an investment that would be lost if she changed direction. Those past years are already gone. Should she continue the rest of her life doing something she hates because she already has spent six years doing something she hates? Those six years have certainly taught her some valuable lessons, which she may be able to apply in a completely new setting. She needs to challenge the belief that changing directions means losing an investment — instead she can use what she has already learned to explore new ways of creating a more satisfying life for herself.

• **Failure is a normal part of life and learning — not a disaster.** Nicole wanted to be a ballet dancer. She had taken ballet lessons through her high school years, and she wanted to go to New York to become a professional ballerina. Her parents, however, thought that her ambition was senseless. They told her, "You can never succeed as a ballerina. Very few do. You don't have the talent. You don't have the body. You will certainly fail if you go to New York." Nicole desperately wanted to try out for the New York Ballet, but she thought, "My parents want the best for me. They must know what I should do. If I tried out and failed, I would be a disgrace to my parents."

Nicole is suffering from the mistaken belief that failure is a disaster. Sure, it is possible, even likely, that Nicole would not be hired by the New York Ballet. Would that constitute a disaster? Only if Nicole sees it that way. A belief that would be more constructive is that the experience of trying out could be an exciting adventure and a great learning experience. Regardless of the outcome, Nicole could have the satisfaction of having given it her best shot, enjoying the process and learning much about show business. And who knows what the very experience of going to New York and trying out might lead to?

RHYMES WITH ORANGE By Hilary B. Price

Examine beliefs that block you from doing your best work.

Some people actually refuse to do their best work to preserve their own self-esteem or to cope with intense pressure from others. Students refuse to study for a final examination so that in case they fail they can say the failure was due to lack of effort, not lack of ability. Other students may refuse to study for the SAT or graduate school entrance examinations as a way of resisting parental pressure to get into a school they don't really desire. This behavior of refusing to do your best work has been called *self-sabotage*. By doing your best work you open up options, but you do not necessarily need to accept the opportunity. You can't learn much about yourself until you try your best. The fear here is that you might learn something you don't want to know. You might learn that you lack some ability or personality characteristic that you consider essential. In fact it is beneficial for you to discover what abilities you currently lack because you can then begin to acquire them. You aren't born knowing everything. You gradually learn throughout life. Thinking of abilities as learned accomplishments will inspire you to do your best and prevent you from sabotaging yourself.

- **You don't need to have a goal to justify maximum effort.** Leon entered college without knowing what he wanted to major in nor what kind of an occupation he eventually wanted to have. He enrolled in courses but seldom studied for tests. He said to his best friend, "As soon as I discover what I really want to do, then I'll buckle down and get to work. Until then, I'm just going to goof off." Leon's behavior is another example of self-sabotage. He applied for several on-campus jobs but was turned down because the recommendations he received from professors were lukewarm. He never tried to master any of the courses he took and so never developed any passion toward them.

Leon had the mistaken belief that "goals" materialize out of thin air and wait to be discovered. He did not realize that people *formulate* their goals as they throw themselves enthusiastically into a variety of activities. Half-hearted efforts are not the way to create goals. Goals can change depending on experiences with related activities. Leon would be better off if he tried to do his very best in whatever courses or activities he entered. In that way he would earn a reputation for persistence and might well discover his passion.

An Exercise in Overcoming Self-Sabotage

To overcome beliefs that may be sabotaging you, you need first to identify your own beliefs and assumptions that may be related.*

1. Do you believe that you are entitled to a well-paying job because of your education?
    ___ Yes ___ No

2. If "Yes," what belief would be more realistic for you now?
    _____
    _____
    _____

3. Do you believe that you can't change your occupation now because you have already invested so much in your training and experience?
    ___ Yes ___ No

---

* *You may be interested in the* Career Beliefs Inventory, *a paper-and-pencil test that helps you identify beliefs that block effective career actions. If you wish, you could take that inventory and identify some beliefs that might possibly be blocking you. Contact a career counselor or the publisher,* CPP, 1-800-624-1765, www.cpp-db.com.

4. If "Yes," what belief would be more realistic for you now?

_____

_____

5. Do you believe that any failure would be a total disaster for you?
    ___ Yes ___ No

6. If "Yes," what belief would be more realistic for you now?

_____

_____

7. Do you believe that you first need to specify a goal to justify your giving a maximum effort?
    ___ Yes ___ No

8. If "Yes," what belief would be more realistic for you now?

_____

_____

9. What other beliefs do you hold that may be stopping you from attaining what you want?

_____

_____

_____

10. How would you change your beliefs from question 9 so that they would no longer be blocking you?

_____

_____

_____

Making the Most of Happenstance.

The experiences of Keisha and Nicole and Leon may not seem to apply to you, but if you consider the lessons to be learned from their lives, you may find there's more than meets the eye.

Don't let self-sabotage prevent you from making the most of happenstance in your life and your career. We want you to make the most of all you've learned in this book. To make it even easier for you, we've summed it all up in the final short chapter that follows.

Chapter 10

Remember That Luck Is No Accident

Important Lessons About Creating Luck

No great deed, private or public, has ever been undertaken in a bliss of certainty.

— Leon Wieseltier

Never ask the way from someone who knows, because then you can never get lost.

— Baal Shem Tov

My luck is so bad that if I bought a cemetery, people would stop dying.

— Rodney Dangerfield

What we have before us are some breathtaking opportunities disguised as insolvable problems.

— John Gardner

What are the most important lessons we hope you have learned from this book? Here's the way we see them:

- *You never need to decide what you are going to be in the future.* You may formulate some goals at various times, but those goals are always subject to change as you grow and learn, and as the world changes around you. Better to keep your eyes and mind open at all times.

- *Unplanned events will inevitably have an impact on your career.* Be alert and ready to take advantage of them when they occur.
- *Reality may be offering you better options than you could have dreamed.* As you pursue your dreams, keep that in mind, and stay awake while you're dreaming.
- *Engaging in a variety of activities will help you discover what you like and dislike.* Throw yourself enthusiastically into each activity and give it your best effort.
- *Expect to make mistakes and experience failures.* They provide great learning experiences, and sometimes they lead to even better outcomes than you could have predicted.
- *You can create your own unplanned lucky events* by volunteering your assistance, joining organizations, taking courses, striking up conversations with friends and strangers, surfing the Web, reading books and magazines, and making yourself valuable to others. In short, by engaging actively in life.
- *Every experience is a way to learn.* Each new job is another learning experience — you need not know how to do the job before you accept it.
- *You can discover a variety of activities that are satisfying, even if you are not employed.* Through such activities you can continue to be helpful to others, although not necessarily in the same ways you did before. Later in life, that's even a healthy approach to retirement.
- *Beliefs that keep you open to new ideas and experiences will help you overcome internal obstacles.* Adopt beliefs and engage in activities that make your life rich and satisfying. In the words of Booker T. Washington, "Success is to be measured not so much by the position that one has reached in life as by the obstacles which one has overcome while trying to succeed."

"Always Learning, Always Trying, Always Wondering"

John Gardner, who died in 2002 at the age of eighty-nine, has been called a "secular saint." John Hennessy, the President of Stanford University said, "John Gardner stands as an exemplar of the power

THE FAMILY CIRCUS   By Bil Keane

Find satisfaction in everyday activities.

of one individual to have a positive impact on society." As Secretary of Health, Education and Welfare under President Lyndon Johnson, Gardner was instrumental in enforcing the 1964 Civil Rights Act, launching Medicare, passing the 1965 Elementary and Secondary Education Act, and creating the Corporation for Public Broadcasting. He was the founder of Common Cause, a citizen's advocacy group that was one of the first to recommend campaign finance reform. These are just a few of his many important accomplishments in helping others.

As you reflect about your own life and the impact you would like to have, you might want to read what John Gardner wrote as he reflected on his own life the year before he died:

> *My career had all the straight-line consistency of a tangled ball of yarn. Did I know where I was headed? Absolutely not! Did I plan my career moves in a logical progression? Absolutely not! There was no grand design. I was a California boy, stumbling cheerfully through life, succeeding, falling on my face, picking myself up and plunging ahead, holding onto some simple values, trying to live with a civil heart as someone said, always learning, always trying, always wondering.*

Creating Luck in Your Life

You do not necessarily need to achieve high political office, or business success, or public recognition to make important contributions to the world. Wherever you are, whatever your work, whoever you meet, you have opportunities to demonstrate to the world the kind of person you are. You can perform useful tasks and help other people with your kindness, support and encouragement. It matters not if your career, like John Gardner's, is "a tangled ball of yarn." Keep learning, keep trying, keep wondering.

Annotated Bibliography

Every book is built on previous contributions from many people. Here are just a few of the many references that provide foundations for this book or illustrate its applications.

BOOKS

Austin, J.H. (2003). *Chance, chase, and creativity: The lucky art of novelty*. New York: Columbia University Press.

The ways in which chance contributes to the creative process in biomedical research and brings about novel and useful results.

Benyus, J. (1997). *Biomimicy: Innovation inspired by nature*. New York: Harper Collins.

A book about how we can learn by mimicking nature, e.g., weave like a spider, capture energy from the sun like a leaf, grow food like a prairie.

Bolles, R. N. (2010). *What color is your parachute? 2010: A practical manual for job-hunters and career-changers*. Berkeley: Ten-Speed Press.

The best-selling book on making career decisions and conducting the job search.

Bradley, Bill (1996). *Time present, time past: A memoir*. New York: A. A. Knopf.

Former basketball star, U.S. Senator and presidential candidate describes the unplanned events that influenced his life and career.

Bridges, W. (2003). *Managing transitions: Making the most of change* (2nd Ed.). New York: Perseus Books.

Describes the emotional impact of organizational change on employees and how their reactions can influence their organization.

Bronson, P. (2002). *What should I do with the rest of my life? The true story of people who answered the ultimate question*. New York: Random House.

Best-selling author's look at how individuals have adjusted to career change including many who made "mistakes" and made the best of them.

Chope, R. C. (2000). *Dancing naked: Breaking through the emotional limits that keep you from the job you want*. Oakland, CA: New Harbinger Publications.

Career transition and job search strategy guide discusses how changes in the workplace require people to be more flexible and innovative.

Esty, D. & Winston A. (2009). *Green to gold: How smart companies use environmental strategy to innovate, create value, and build competitive advantage*. Hoboken, NJ: Wiley.

This publication provides a historical, financial and pragmatic analysis of the evolution of business attitudes with respect to environmental responsibility, global warming, and electronic waste.

Figler, H. E. (1999). *The complete job-search handbook: Everything you need to know to get the job you really want*. New York: Owl Books.

Well-known practical guide on the skills necessary for effective job seeking.

Friedman, T. L. (2008). *Hot, flat, and crowded: Why we need a green revolution — and how it can renew America*. New York: Farrar, Straus and Giroux.

A book about how America has been too intent on defining enemies and building walls. What is needed is leadership in building friendships and solving the real problems of people in the world — building a green world with everyone.

Gebhard, N., Marriner, M. with Gordon, J. (2003). *Roadtrip nation: A guide to discovering your path in life*. New York: Ballantine Books.

Written by two twenty-year-olds especially for today's generation of college students and recent college graduates. Describes their "roadtrip" across the United States, and interviews with prominent professionals who experienced unexpected highs and lows on their path to career success.

Hawkins, P. Lovins, A., & Lovins, L.H. (2008). *Natural capitalism: Creating the next industrial revolution*. Lebanon, IN: Back Bay Books.

The authors describe how leading-edge businesses are practicing a new version of industrialism that is efficient and profitable and concerned with the environment and creating jobs.

Kinnier, R. T. (2001). *The point of it all*. North Chelmsford, MA: Erudition Books.

A readable analysis of how various wise people have construed the meaning of life.

Kinnier, R. T., Kernes, J. L., Tribbensee, N. E., & VanPuymbroeck, C. M. (Eds.) (2006). *The meaning of life, according to the great and the good*. Bath, England: Palazzo Editions, Ltd.

In response to the centuries-old question, "What is the meaning of life?" this book presents the answers given by some of the most respected and well-known philosophers, theologians, writers, and eminent people in the world. They don't all agree.

Levin, A. S., Krumboltz, J. D., & Krumboltz, B. L. (1993). *A workbook for exploring your career beliefs*. Palo Alto, CA: Consulting Psychologists Press.

Useful companion to the Career Beliefs Inventory. This user-friendly workbook provides concise descriptions of the 25 "career belief" scales most important for career satisfaction, as well as exercises to help you overcome career barriers.

Llewellyn, A. B., Hendrix, J. P. & Golden, K.C. (2008). *Green jobs: A guide to eco-friendly employment*. Avon, Mass.: Adams Media.

"Earth-friendly living is no longer an option or a virtuous sacrifice; it's an obligation." The authors see green employment as a way out of unemployment and sub-wage employment.

McDonough, W. & Braungart, M. (2002). *Cradle to cradle: Remaking the way we make things*. New York: North Point Press.

This book makes a strong case concerning the idea that businesses can be both profitable and concerned with the environment and provides several specific examples from the corporate world.

ARTICLES

Bandura, A. (1982). The psychology of chance encounters and life paths. *American Psychologist*, 37, 747–755.

Points out the important role of chance events in shaping the course of life and suggests personal and social determinants of their impact.

Baumgardner, S.R. (1982). Coping with disillusionment, abstract images, and uncertainty in career decision making. *Personnel and Guidance Journal*, 61, 213–217.

Suggests that systematic planning is minimally related to either career choice or finding a job, but that friends, prior employment and chance circumstances are more frequently involved.

Betsworth, D. G., & Hansen, J-I. C. (1996). The categorization of serendipitous career development events. *Journal of Career Assessment*, 4, 91–98.

A study showing that about 60% of senior adults from 52 to 88 years old credited serendipitous events as having a significant influence on their careers.

Blustein, D.L. (1997). A context-rich perspective of career exploration across the life role. *Career Development Quarterly*, 45, 260–274.

Advocates that exploratory activities have benefits beyond the career arena — for example in citizenship, homemaking, academic, and leisure roles.

Cabral, A.C., & Salomone, P.R. (1990). Chance and careers: Normative versus contextual development. *Career Development Quarterly*, 39, 5–17.

Advocates that students develop a sensitivity to both planned and unforeseen events and an ability to evaluate and act on options when faced with potential change.

Dorn, F. J. (1988). Utilizing social influence in career counseling: A case study. *Career Development Quarterly*, 36, 269–281.

Illustrates how career clients can learn to attribute their difficulties to factors over which they actually have some control.

Gelatt, H.B. (1989). Positive uncertainty: A new decision-making framework for counseling. *Journal of Counseling Psychology*, 36, 252-256.

Advocates acceptance of open-mindedness as a desirable attitude in facing the inevitable uncertainties of the future.

Hart, D.H., Rayner, K., & Christensen, E.R. (1971). Planning, preparation, and chance in occupational entry. *Journal of Vocational Behavior*, 1, 279–285.

A study of sixty adult males, finding that professional employees tended to attribute their careers to planning, while skilled and semi-skilled employees were more likely to identify chance as a major influence.

Hornak, J., & Gillingham, B. (1980). Career indecision: a self-defeating behavior. *Personnel and Guidance Journal*, 59, 252–253.

Suggests that, since most career choices are not permanent, students can overcome their fears by learning to engage in career exploration.

Krieshok, T. S. (2001). How the decision-making literature might inform career center practice. *Journal of Career Development*, 27, 207–216.

Advocates less emphasis on getting decided and more emphasis on developing an inquiring and adaptive attitude toward work.

Krumboltz, J.D. (1979). A social learning theory of career decision making. Revised and reprinted in A.M. Mitchell, G.B. Jones, and J.D. Krumboltz (Eds.), *Social Learning and Career Decision Making* (pp. 19–49). Cranston, RI: Carroll Press.

Career decisions are based on uncountable numbers of learning experiences, occurring in both intentional and unplanned ways, and resulting from encounters in schools, libraries, work settings, family contacts, unions, religious organizations, and other settings.

Krumboltz, J.D. (1992). The wisdom of indecision. *Journal of Vocational Behavior*, 41, 239–244.

Proposes a number of benefits associated with remaining "open-minded" instead of being "decisive."

Krumboltz, J.D. (1999). *Career Beliefs Inventory: Applications and technical guide*. Palo Alto, CA: Consulting Psychologists Press.

Description of the Career Beliefs Inventory, an assessment instrument designed to identify beliefs and assumptions that may either block or facilitate career satisfaction.

Krumboltz, J.D. (2009). The happenstance learning theory. *Journal of Career Assessment*, 17, 135–154. DOI: 10.1177/1069072708328861.

An explanation of how people can create important unplanned beneficial events by taking appropriate actions. The goal is to help people develop a more satisfying life — not merely to make a career decision. Outcomes should be ascertained from people's real-world activities — not from the counseling dialogue.

Miller, M. J. (1983). The role of happenstance in career choice. *The Vocational Guidance Quarterly*, 32, 16–20.

Attention to unplanned events is important because most people do not attribute their vocational choices to a rational decision-making process.

Mitchell, K. E., Levin, A. S., & Krumboltz, J. D. (1999). Planned happenstance: Constructing unexpected career opportunities, *Journal of Counseling and Development*, 77, 115–124.

Explains how counselors can help people learn to create unexpected career opportunities and benefit from them.

Salomone, P. R., & Slaney, R. B. (1981). The influence of chance and contingency factors on the vocational choice process of nonprofessional workers. *Journal of Vocational Behavior*, 19, 25–35.

An early article published on the influence of chance on career choice.

Savickas, M. L. (1997). Career adaptability: An integrative construct for life-span, life-space theory. *Career Development Quarterly*, 45, 247–259.

Suggests that adaptability — flexibility in responding to the environment — is an important component of career development.

Scott, J., & Hatalla, J. (1990) The influence of chance and contingency factors on career patterns of college-educated women. *Career Development Quarterly*, 39, 18–30.

A study showing the two-thirds of the college-educated sample identified "unexpected personal events" as influencing their careers.

Smith, J. (2002). The 5 secrets of good luck: It's not about chance — it's about making life go your way. *Redbook Magazine*, January 2002, 50–52.

Celebrity stories about creating good luck, as well as comments by the authors of *Luck Is No Accident*.

Watts, A. G. (1996). Toward a policy for lifelong career development: A transatlantic perspective. Career Development Quarterly, 45, 41–53.

Advocates a lifelong "planful serendipity" strategy of encouraging individuals to set trajectories for themselves but to revise them frequently as new possibilities arise.

Watts, A. G. (1999). Reshaping career development for the 21st century. *http://www.derby.ac.uk/files/icegs_reshaping_career_development1999a.pdf*

Tony Watts presents the view from England that career counseling should capitalize more on the chance events that affect everyone's life. His view is quite compatible with the Happenstance Learning Theory.

Williams, E. N., Soeprapto, E., Like, K. Touradji, P., Hess, S., & Hill, C. E. (1998). Perceptions of serendipity: Career paths of prominent women in counseling psychology. *Journal of Counseling Psychology*, 45, 379–389.

A study describing how chance events influenced the careers of thirteen prominent female counseling psychologists.

Young, J.B., & Rodgers, R.F (1997). A model of radical career change in the context of psychosocial development. *Journal of Career Assessment*, 5, 167–182.

A study of ten professionals who successfully made major career changes after agonizing over external and internal factors that resisted change.

Career and Green-Job Websites

Bureau of Labor Statistics http://www.bls.gov/oco/cgindex.htm
Website for the principal fact-finding agency for the U.S. Federal Government in the area of labor economics and statistics including information about training and advancement, earnings, job prospects, and working conditions.

California Career Zone http://www.cacareerzone.org/graphic/index.html
This website helps individuals explore a multitude of occupations in California through self-assessment exercises, videos of occupations of interest, and a "Reality Check" game comparing an individual's lifestyle needs with specific salary information in different locations.

Career InfoNet http://www.careerinfonet.org
This website provides occupation and industry information, salary data, career videos, education resources, self-assessment activities and tools, and other resources for today's fast-paced global marketplace.

Career Voyages http://www.careervoyages.gov/index.cfm
This website is a collaboration between the Department of Labor and the Department of Education. It provides information on high growth, in-demand occupations and the skills and educational requirements for these positions.

Government Grants http://www.grants.gov
Need a government grant? Here is where you find out how to get one. You can also find job opportunities made available by the Recovery Act where you can search by job title and location.

Green Career Central http://www.greencareercentral.com
A membership organization which does provide some free information about green careers. You can learn how to explore your green career possibilities, the most popular green career options, and how to take effective action.

Green Collar Blog http://www.greencollarblog.org
Provides a comprehensive listing of job boards that focus on social or environmental responsibility, the hidden green job market, and future green jobs.

Jim Cassio http://www.cassio.com
Jim Cassio provides consulting services and workshops on green jobs and careers. He also makes available a free Green Careers Resource Guide.

Occupational Outlook Handbook http://www.bls.gov/oco
The Occupational Outlook Handbook has been a nationally recognized source of helpful career information and is now available in this on-line version of the original

publication. This resource summarizes and categorizes many career fields to aid in exploration and is updated every two years.

O*NET Online http://online.onetcenter.org
This on-line program is a primary source of occupational information providing a database of career exploration tools, assessments, and other resources for both job changers and students looking to investigate numerous occupations.

RoadTrip Nation http://www.roadtripnation.com
A book, DVD series, and this website were developed by recent college graduates who sought to identify and explore career opportunities in a non-traditional way. They proceeded to travel the United States and interviewed successful people in a variety of occupational areas to learn about the planned and unplanned events that influenced their careers.

Sloan Career Cornerstone Center http://www.careercornerstone.org/index.htm
This website was funded by the Alfred P. Sloan Foundation to provide a resource center for individuals exploring careers in science, technology, engineering, mathematics, computing, and healthcare.

U.S. Department of Labor Statistics http://www.bls.gov
Provides current articles on changes in the labor market and resources for job seekers, consumers, investors and business leaders. Information is also tailored for separate regions of the country. "Career Information for Kids" is another feature.

U.S.A. Government Jobs http://www.usa.gov
A useful way to search for government jobs by job title and location. Access to federal, state, local, military and volunteer jobs is available along with information about student aid, insurance coverage, the Peace Corps, and workplace issues.

The White House http://www.whitehouse.gov
Hear the latest news from the President of the United States and reports on current legislative issues. Issues include civil rights, education, energy, jobs, environment, health, poverty, and technology.

Workforce One http://www.workforce3one.org
An e-learning, knowledge sharing webspace that offers workforce professionals, employers, economic development, and education professionals a dynamic network featuring innovative workforce solutions. Online learning events, resource information, and tools help organizations learn how to develop strategies that enable individuals and businesses to be successful in the 21st century economy.

Yahoo's Hot Jobs/Green Jobs http://hotjobs.yahoo.com/jobs-c-green
Yahoo provides thousands of green (and other) job offerings which you can search by keywords, city, state, zip code and job category.

Websites courtesy of the Sacramento State University Career Center and Linda Kobylarz and Associates, Burlington, Connecticut.

Index

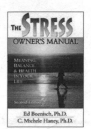
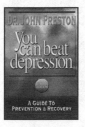
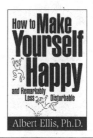

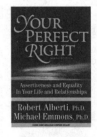
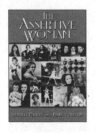